One thing most people want more of is confidence. Consider this your how-to guide to feel and project confidence in all situations.

Flaunting requires you to notice your wins, feel proud of them, and share them out loud with others. To do that, you need to overcome barriers by quieting the voices that quiet you (including your own), looking at language that helps or hinders how you're perceived, and applying your new, confident self to challenging situations like navigating power dynamics.

These problems aren't new. Landry's solutions are.

Flaunt will develop your confidence from the inside out. Get reading. Eureka moments await!

Flaunt
Radiate Confidence Your Way

Brenda Landry

Rock's Mills Press
Rock's Mills, Ontario • Oakville, Ontario
2024

Published by
Rock's Mills Press
www.rocksmillspress.com

Copyright © 2024, 2023 by Brenda Landry. All rights reserved.
This book may not be reproduced, in whole or in part,
without the written permission of the publisher.

Author photograph by Viktoriia Musiienko.

For information about this title, including retail, adoption,
and bulk orders as well as permissions requests,
please contact the publisher at customer.service@rocksmillspress.com.

I dedicate this book to my father for gifting me with confidence,
my mother for the skills to write about it,
and my sister for being my biggest supporter
in completing this book—and in all things.

Contents

Preface • ix

CHAPTER 1
It's All You • 3

CHAPTER 2
We're All Faking It • 17

CHAPTER 3
Bad Words • 31

CHAPTER 4
Good Words • 49

CHAPTER 5
After Hours • 59

CHAPTER 6
Sticky Situations • 77

CHAPTER 7
Kraft Dinner • 97

CHAPTER 8
Helpful Advice • 115

CHAPTER 9
You, Out Loud • 133

CHAPTER 10
Flaunt Your Face Off • 149

Acknowledgements • 167

Works Cited • 169

Preface

Thanks for picking up this book. Ideally you've already bought it, but if you're still wondering whether you should, I'm going to give you some compelling reasons to do so. Look, I know, another book about empowering women and building confidence (insert eye roll here), but here's the thing: unfortunately, it is still needed.

When I began working in the field of gender diversity over a decade ago, I knew the firm I was interviewing with offered women's leadership development programs, and that I'd be expected to teach them. I openly cautioned my hopefully future boss that I wasn't sure how good I'd be because I didn't really believe it was needed or that segregating women into "special classes" was the way to go. I mean, aren't we past that yet? I hadn't experienced a ton of gender bias (or so I thought), and of course, I assumed my experience was the same for all other women on the planet (nice assumption, Brenda). My hopefully future boss chuckled and said, "Well, why don't you sit in on a session as a participant, and then we can chat?" I did, and within 15 minutes of the beginning of the two-day course, I was converted. What I learned was that there are undeniably gender-specific traits that stand in the way of us being seen and heard as leaders. While I've seen these traits in men, they are overwhelmingly apparent in women. Things like speaking quietly, making ourselves small, and weakening our ideas with disclaimers and apologies—all behaviours that were instilled in us through our upbringing and other means of social conditioning, and all behaviours that can be modified through increased courage and confidence.

For those of you who need more than a short story to be convinced this book is still needed, here's some data. A 2019 report tells us that worldwide gender equality is still 95 years away. The report analyzed 153 countries in their progress toward gender parity, focusing on four main themes: economic participation, educational attainment, health and survival, and political empowerment. The number of women in senior leadership and board positions has barely budged in the past two decades. There are books and courses and consultants who focus on addressing the systemic wrongs that create this disparity at the organizational and societal levels; however, this book was written for you. You've likely heard the expression, "Be the change you wish to see in the world," and while some may see this as a form of victim-blaming, I see it as empowering the disempowered. I don't know who taught you that you should quiet your power, that your ideas don't matter, or that flaunting your abilities was unseemly, but this book is going to try very hard to undo those messages. I've dedicated much of my career to this mission, but since there are a finite number of two-day courses I can teach in my remaining years, I needed to find a way to bring these lessons to a larger audience in a shorter amount of time. There is still a long way to go, and I don't have 95 years.

The purpose of this book is to help you shake off your insecurities, quiet your fears, and bring you back to you, the full, powerful, strong, smart you who already has all that you need to be the best version of yourself.

You're going to find that the book is written in an unfiltered way. I'm not going to gloss over the tough issues or sugarcoat the solutions. I've written this in a raw and genuine way. I wasn't striving for perfection; I was shooting for my personal best—a lesson you'll learn in the coming pages. I've made some assertions that are contentious, and you may disagree with me on occasion. Fact is, I've been specializing in this area for a long time, and the stories and lessons I offer are the result of my experience. That said, I do acknowledge my experience has limitations. I am fully aware of my privilege. I'm a white, educated, childless woman who comes from a middle-class family that valued learning and socialization, and those realities significantly shape the way I am received in this world and the opportunities I am afforded.

This book is dedicated to my father, Pat Landry, who apparently did the opposite of most dads: he nurtured an unapologetically confident daughter. He cheered on the young (and old-er) performer in me; he celebrated my wins and showed compassion for my losses; he role-modeled confidence like no one I've ever seen; and he told me, in a way I completely believed, that I could do and be absolutely anything I wanted in this world. In 2011 he asked me what his legacy would be when he was gone (since neither my sister nor I had children), and I didn't have an answer. I felt some sadness for him, and it stayed with me. Shortly after, I was on a mountaintop in Honduras, working with women to help them grow into their own power, and one of them asked me how I became so confident. It was in that moment that my father's legacy became as clear as the stars above me. I would continue his mission in another way: I'd share the gift that my father gave to me with as many people as possible in my remaining years. It would and has become my calling, my life's mission, and my father's legacy. On March 9, 2018, my father passed away, but his love and inspiration still run through me and have fueled every word I've written in this book. I'm thrilled to share him with you.

Simply reading the book will likely fire you up, but I want more than that. I want you to fundamentally change the way you think and feel about yourself and change the way you show up in the world. Truth is, I'm aiming to create a movement here. A movement where everyone feels and flaunts their best selves, because when that happens, the world becomes a better place. When that happens, we'll see more gender equity, more balance in leadership, and a more diverse range of decision-makers. When that happens, we'll see more compassion and humanity in the world.

Flaunt

CHAPTER 1

It's All You

"Secure your own mask first, before helping others."

"Pay yourself first."

"Practice self-love."

We hear it all. It makes sense. I mean, logically, if we're dead, poor, or otherwise deflated, how can we possibly be any good to others? Wait ... why did that shift to "others" so quickly??!? There's something about women that drives us to be "of service" to others. To help others. To nurture others. Whatever it is that causes us to be this way ... I have it, and most of you probably do, too.

It's not pure, altruistic selflessness. We get something from it. Come on—it feels good to help others! But here's the concerning part ... it feels even better when we help others at the expense of ourselves. Our sacrifice of self is part of it. That *is* concerning! We are getting something out of depriving ourselves of our own wants and needs. The concern is the risks that this can cause. Those risks can range from feeling resentful for not feeling fulfilled, to losing ourselves in other's problems, to finding ourselves in abusive relationships. It's not uncommon for people to wake up one day to realize they were living for others instead of living their own lives, and then make drastic changes that disrupt not only their lives, but the lives of others—for good or bad.

This chapter isn't going to try to turn us all into self-serving people who stop helping others. In fact, quite the opposite. This chapter will argue that the risks of not having a balance between helping others and helping yourself are significant enough to compel you to try another way. And the other way I'm talking about—having balance—will actually lift you to a place where you have more energy, more focus, and more positivity to help others. Loving yourself, taking care of yourself, is not selfish. It's not saying "Me first." It's saying "Me too."

Very few women I know put themselves first (or second, or third … or fourth). I alluded to this above, but here's the naked truth … I am not qualified to be writing on this topic. You see, I have not figured this out. I am a work-in-progress. And, frankly, I'm still in the beginning stages. Don't get me wrong; I *do* love myself. I do. But for some extremely annoying reason, I find myself doing things that don't bring me joy, that aren't good for me. I find myself not only in relationships with dysfunctional people but drawn to them. It all leaves me drained. And the worst part is, I'm not filling myself back up.

Now, before you think I'm hopeless, I will say that I've gotten much better at that last part. For the past two years, I've been working with a therapist, and I am proud to say I am the *best* patient I'm sure she's ever had. I really am. I was so determined to stop these harmful patterns that I literally did everything she suggested I do. She said, maybe start taking a few vitamins (to help regulate my hormones/moods), so I immediately drove to Costco and bought every vitamin she suggested. She emphasized the importance of exercise in self-care, so I immediately started running (OK, jogging) and boxing again. She asked me what kind of emotional outlet worked for me in the past, and I told her about playing the piano as a teenager and working out my emotions on the keys. She said nothing more. I'm sure you know where I'm going with this. Yes, I now own a secondhand upright concert grand piano.

While all of this was going on, I was working hard to detach myself from a toxic relationship. A painful detachment. And I needed guidance on how to come back into myself. My therapist had her hands full. She quickly recognized that I was in an unhealthy, codependent relationship. That I had lost myself in the coupledom. That I had stopped taking care of myself, which so many of us women do. By the way, these unhealthy relationships can also exist with friends and family.

I never stopped loving myself, but I was treating me like shit. I mean, if I treated other people the way I was treating myself, I'm sure I would have no friends. Who would stick around for someone who spends no time with them and has no regard for what they want?! Honestly, some of us probably treat our acquaintances better than we treat ourselves.

I decided it was time. Time I worked on showing myself how special and amazing I was. Time to romance myself (not that way … well sometimes, maybe ;) …). Time to express my love of myself to myself. I always secretly wished someone loved me the way I loved others. I fancy myself to be quite a fabulous lover. I spoil the people I love. I make them beautiful dinners, run gorgeous bubble baths with candles and wine, take them on trips, plan fun excursions, and tell them often how special they are. Really, they are quite lucky, and I am jealous of them. So, it was time. It was *my* time. For the first time in my life, I was going to put myself on the receiving end of my love.

This was a drastic change.

I love others so deeply that I honestly didn't care what we did, where we ate, what movie we watched ... as long as I was with them. Aw. Cute. But not really. This deferential attitude was dangerous, because after years of being this way, I had actually lost the ability to tap into what I truly did want and need! I'm kind of ashamed to say, but I felt like I didn't even have wants or needs anymore. *I had lost myself.* That expression is real, and it happened to me.

I thought loving people this way—putting others first and ignoring my own needs—was what true love was all about. I'm sure you can imagine my disappointment when the men I was with didn't reciprocate in the same way. My partners would say what they wanted, and minutes later, we'd be doing it (get your mind out of the gutter). And I used to resent that! I used to think they were being selfish because they actually said what they wanted. And I was insecure about their love, because if they were putting themselves first, to me that meant they were putting me second. Which is not what I do when I show love. I put them first. So, let's take a count here. I put them first, they put them first ... soooooo ... who puts me first? Truth is, I was envious. I now know that what I was doing was unhealthy love.

There seems to be a fear that when women love themselves, it will come at a cost of our ability to love others. Perhaps that's why it's considered a bad thing, but regardless, it's most definitely a suppression of something that is not only OK, it's *necessary*. Without practicing self-love, we lack the confidence conditioning needed to project the fullest, best version of ourselves, and *that* is a legitimate thing to fear.

My objective is to get you to love yourself unconditionally—and why not? Why not?!?! We have people we love unconditionally: our partners, families, friends. This unconditional love we give so generously to others is full of acceptance and forgiveness and is unwavering. Doesn't it sound amazing? It does, so it's time we give some of that good stuff to ourselves. Like our love for others, we have to love ourselves *always*. It's not enough to only love ourselves when we win or look good; we must also love ourselves when we've failed, made mistakes, and look or feel bad. I'll use my delightful sister for this example because she can do no wrong in my eyes. Let's pretend my sister made a mistake (ha ha, it is rare).

Many years ago, our family was in Seattle to watch a major league baseball game. We all got ready, headed down to the ballfield, and eagerly approached the will-call window, where we all fully expected to find the tickets that my usually-exceptionally-gifted-planner sister purchased. Turns out, the tickets weren't there. I can't even remember why. Did my parents and I turn resentful toward her? Stop loving her? Not for a second. She'd made a mistake, and in the very same moment, we forgave her. Sadly, she didn't forgive herself quite as quickly. She is forever safe in our love for her. This is the kind of love we all deserve from ourselves. It's OK, and even encouraged, to learn from our mistakes and seek to improve our weak spots, but I'm asking you all right now to do so through a healthy lens of self-acceptance, self-compassion, and self-love.

You know yourself. You know the good and the bad, the strong and the weak, the beautiful and ugly parts of you. I'm not always proud of my words or actions, but I *refuse* to break up with myself. I heard a radio interview with a lovely couple who were celebrating their 75th wedding anniversary. The interviewer asked them their secret of staying married for so long. Their answer was simple—divorce wasn't an option back then. For most of their marriage, it was literally impossible for them to *not* be married. I'm sure there were many times when they let each other down, made mistakes, or hurt each other in some way, yet here they were 75 years later, still in love. I could hear it through the airwaves. So, I invite you to enter into a committed, lifelong love affair with yourself, one where, no matter what happens, you'll always love yourself.

I've worked with thousands of women from all around the globe. What astonishes me is, regardless of where we are in the world, or what industry we're in, or what role we have, or how much education we have, we all want to have more confidence. Many excellent books have been dedicated to improving confidence, and perhaps this is another, but very few get to the root of the matter. Confidence is a feeling which can and should be projected, but ultimately, it is a feeling. A feeling that is generated inside of you.

These days, more than ever, we seek validation from others rather than our internal sources, and I want you to work on shifting that. How many of you jump on Facebook or Instagram and look for how many "likes" (or, even better, "loves") your post got? What about praise from a boss or co-worker? External validation is a social norm; it happens, and trust me, I want you to "love" this book, but counting on external validation alone is dangerous because it's unreliable and, in its absence, we may feel deflated and unloved. That's why we need to have our confidence rooted much deeper than that, in self-love.

I've heard it's unbecoming to love yourself. It's conceited and arrogant. Frankly, I've never heard of anything more absurd. Ever. This book is my contribution towards a movement of squashing such foolishness. Seriously, fuck that. If it's wrong to love myself, I don't want to be right. I guess the greatest offense would be loving myself out loud—expressing my love of myself. Well, as you can probably tell by the title of this book, I'm all about flaunting. I'm often told by friends that they love my confidence. I'm often booked to speak to groups of women because I exude confidence. I'm some people's favourite person to be around because I am unapologetically confident. Sometimes my flaunting is so bold, it gets a laugh, and I've thought a lot about that. Does the audience think I'm being funny? Are they uncomfortable? Having asked for a lot of feedback, I can tell you that rather than making people uncomfortable, it seems my confidence inspires others to feel free to do the same. I give others permission to demonstrate self-love and to flaunt it. The laughter seems to be a feeling of joy, having witnessed something that is, unfortunately, uncommon to see: a truly confident woman.

I'm interested in you developing unconditional confidence, meaning not only "I feel confident when…" or "I feel confident if…" but an unwavering confidence. Where does humility come in? Isn't it good to be humble? Of course, and I can guarantee you are. Think about confidence and humility as muscles in your body. Confidence is your bicep, and humility is your tricep—both need to be developed for your arm to function well. Now, imagine that one of these muscles is very weak and the other very strong. How would your arm work? That's right: poorly. A personal trainer would immediately begin working with you on strengthening your bicep. That's what I'm doing—focusing on the area that needs strengthening: your confidence.

Put simply, never in my 15 years of practicing in this area have I had to coach a woman to be humbler. Not once. Trust me, I look forward to the day when more humility is needed, and I get to write the sequel to this book, *How to Become Humbler*.

Now that you're convinced that loving yourself is healthy, let's heat up this romance. Like every relationship, it starts with the words you say.

Answer these questions:

Who do you talk to the most in a day?

Who do you trust more than anyone else?

Who did you name? Because the correct answer to both is *you*.

Think about it. We talk to ourselves all day. That's fine; it's normal; but here's the freaky thing: there is no one in this world you trust more than yourself. This means that everything you say to yourself you immediately believe to be the truth. Get that? Your brain doesn't see the need to apply a filter to determine how much of what it's hearing is true when it's coming from you. This should both scare the shit out of you and present an opportunity. Really, this shows you the power of self-talk. If you say something negative about yourself, you immediately believe it as the truth. *And*, when you say something positive about yourself, you immediately believe it as the truth. Lesson here? Choose your words carefully when talking to yourself.

I've worked with thousands of women, and I often ask them to write down negative phrases they say to themselves. What I hear back is really sad. It's true and honest, but my goodness, is it *sad*. "No one is going to take you seriously; you're too young." "You look fat in that dress." "Your idea is stupid, and no one wants to hear it." Most of us would never let someone else talk to us like that. Yet these phrases have become our internal soundtracks, our default, what we're most comfortable hearing ourselves say. If this book accomplishes nothing but make you be more kind to yourself through self-talk, writing it will have been worth it for me. Seriously.

Changing your internal monologue to one that is more kind takes awareness and intention. It is absolutely imperative that your positive self-talk outweighs your negative self-talk by a ratio of two-to-one. To illustrate the solution, I'll give you an analogy. I worked with a personal trainer for a while (a short while; she wanted me at the gym at 5 a.m.), and she made me stand on one of those evil scales that somehow can read a concerning amount of what was happening inside me. At one point, I thought I'd even have my future told by this thing. Anyway, one data point it spit out was how much water was in my body, which was apparently not enough. My trainer began grilling me about my water intake, and I proudly told her how much water I drink. Then she asked how much coffee I drink in a day; that is when shit got real. Was she about to tell me (at 5 a.m. on a Monday) that I couldn't drink coffee anymore? Because I'm not sure being fit was worth that. Thankfully, no. She just wanted to make sure I understood that coffee is a diuretic and that coffee intake cancels out water intake. So, for every cup of coffee I drink, I need to replenish the water loss AND add to my hydration, which means two glasses of water. So, in case you're struggling with math here, the formula is:

1 cup of coffee = 2 glasses of water.

OK, back to self-talk. When you deliver yourself negative self-talk, it damages your self-esteem. Since we want to build self-esteem, we need to follow the coffee/water formula, but serving ourselves two doses of positive self-talk for every negative one. One serving to replenish the hit from the negative talk, and one to build your self-esteem. Again, here's the formula:

1 negative self-talk = 2 positive self-talk.

Here's an example: if you catch yourself saying, "My idea sucks, so I should keep my mouth closed," you need to offset that with two positives, something like, "My idea offers a starting point for a good conversation," *and* "My ideas are mostly well-received, I will take a chance!"

Part of taking care of yourself is knowing where to put your energy. This means saying no to activities that you don't want to do, and spending time only with people who give as much as they take from you. We are busy people! And we only have so much energy and time in a day, so I say spend it wisely. Think of it like this: You have an energy bucket. It fills and it empties. Only you know the level it's at, and therefore, only you are able to make decisions to ensure it's full enough to keep going or if it needs refilling.

Imagine this: you've been invited to a ladies' "paint night." You know what I mean. Everyone drinks wine and is coached through how to paint the same picture as everyone else in the room. You don't really want to go; you've had a long day, and really, all you want is to curl up with your dog and a great book (like this one). But you feel you *should* go. I mean, it's being organized by Shelley, and she always attends your events. Plus, it's a fundraiser for her kid's gymnastics club. Oh, *and* your mother-in-law will be there. Wow—three compelling reasons to go. You really *should* go. But the truth is, you've had a long week at work and you're feeling tired (your energy bucket is very low). You want and need some rest. The fact is, most of us will go to the damn paint night because the alternative is to either tell Shelley you're not going because you'd rather stay home alone or—much more likely—you'll make up some excuse (i.e., lie). Because simply saying no and saying we're taking care of ourselves tonight sounds *so* insane that we fear others wouldn't understand. Yes, this is how crazy we've become.

Now, let's look at who we're choosing to spend our time with. We've all had friends who motivate us, challenge us, bring us joy, and make us laugh. Let's call them "givers." We also have all had friends who are exhausting. You know the ones; they are negative, require a great deal from you, often complain about something, or are wrapped up in some drama. Let's call them "takers." Here's the thing: to both of these friends, you are giving, and in only one of these scenarios is someone giving back to you. Of course, if your "taker" is in a temporary funk or is going through a crisis, it would be wrong to abandon them—they need you to give and they need to take from you. That's fine; we've all been that person, and so this works out as a balanced relationship in the long run. However, if the taker is consistently taking, and it's their pattern to do so, I suggest you ask yourself what value you are getting from this relationship. Sounds harsh, maybe even cold, perhaps even selfish, but these people are draining your energy bucket and that energy drain could eventually start to impact other areas of your life (career, sleep, exercise, other relationships).

Here's a way you can assess whether your current relationships are givers or takers. Ask yourself this: after spending an afternoon with this person, do you feel uplifted or do you feel like you need a nap? As I mentioned, we tend to want to take care of and nurture others. This is a wonderful quality many of us have. But it is also one that must be carefully monitored because if we are constantly walking through our lives with drained buckets, we will get sick. We will deflate. We will be no good to anyone.

Once you've decided to stop spending time on activities that don't bring you joy and with people who are draining your energy, you will likely need some help on how to start actually doing this. I'm getting better at this, and my coach has been my sister, Gillian. Gillian has this ability to listen carefully to others' complex life stories, show compassion and empathy, and then establish boundaries around how and to what degree she will be involved in taking on their problems (spoiler alert: usually not at all). Her famous line is, "Well, good luck with that." She says it to me all the time. And I respect the hell out of her for it.

Now, imagine you've carved out a night for yourself. Ahhhh! How lovely. Now, what to do?

Well, what are the things that fill your bucket? Here are a few of mine:

- Go see live music
- Pampering

- Spa
- Bath time (candles and wine included)
- Dancing
- Cooking
- And eating
- Reading
- *The Bachelor*
  - The series
  - Real life bachelors ;)
- Shopping
- Hiking with my adorable dog (a yellow lab)
- Going to the beach
- Going to the gym
- Visiting friends
- Going to the movies

Me on a hot date with me. I love this selfie. It became my online dating profile picture. It captures a moment where I was taking care of myself, and that's something I want a partner to get used to.

I found myself single in the summer. *So* much to do! And I have friends—lots of them. But it does happen that sometimes none of them are available to hang out on a given night. So, what's a girl to do? Well. This might be mind-blowing. But I don't see one thing on my list that requires another person to be with me! I can do all these things alone. And I have.

When is the last time you took yourself on a date? Gone to a movie by yourself, gone out for a drink or dinner by yourself, gone to the beach by yourself, gone dancing by yourself? Some would say this is cliché, and we've all read this before, but how many of you have actually done it?

I took myself out on a really fabulous date one night. I went to a night market in the north end of Halifax. Bought myself a beer. Bought myself a five-dollar bracelet, which broke six minutes later. Then I walked down to a lovely restaurant, sat on their gorgeous outdoor patio, and had oysters and champagne. The main stage of the Jazz Festival was right across the street, and I had a front row seat. One might even say a VIP seat (I mean, I did have champagne).

Here's the deal: Whether or not people want to participate in your life experiences shouldn't dictate what experiences you have in your life.

Please remember: no one knows what you need more than you. When you need a day off, when you need a hug, when you need help.

Take care of yourself.

CHAPTER 2

We're All Faking It

I'm perfectly imperfect. So are you. We all are!

Perfectionism is like an evil drug; it promises an unattainable high that keeps us coming back for more. We got hooked through a false narrative about its existence, and society is our dealer. Women battle this addiction far more than men.

Perfectionism is an aspiration that requires a comparison. In other words, to see perfection, you must know what it looks like. If perfection is unattainable, how is it possible to witness it? Perhaps your picture of perfection is drawn by pulling together elements of people who you hold in high regard, like parents, teachers, or famous people. It's likely there isn't one single person who possesses all of the traits you've determined make up the perfect person. If you have found someone, I hate to burst your bubble, but you're glorifying someone beyond their limits. I have been guilty of this. I see the best in people; I like all people and have been told I see the world through rose-coloured glasses. These are traits I love about myself: I'm an optimistic, positive person who is confident enough to know and appreciate my strengths yet humble enough to believe everyone else has their unique strengths, too. I don't really want to stop being this way, but these traits can often become blinders. I'll often miss "red flags," or trust too easily, which can be unsafe for me. The reality is that, while everyone has strengths, we all have weaknesses, too. This balance makes us human, and loving the strong and weak parts of ourselves is what's needed for true self-love.

Like much of what I know, this lesson came to me through a personal experience. I had my first real taste of love as a teenager. Admittedly, I knew very little about love at that time, but he was sweet, and cool, and fun, so it was love. We lost touch with each other for about 20 years, and during that time, I had put him on such a pedestal that, if it were up to me, there'd be a statue of him somewhere. In my mind, he was perfect. When we reconnected years later, the first thing I asked was for him to please tell me something wrong with him, so I could be released from holding him in such high regard. That's when he told me about his addiction and that he was 47 days clean. In that very moment, I felt shame. Who was I to put him on that pedestal? He never asked for that. It was unfair of me to see him as perfect, because doing so set an expectation on him. Through that four-hour call, he became human to me—perfectly imperfect—and I loved him even more for it.

There's danger in perfection. Real danger. To show this, I'm going to share another true story, and as you read it, remember that the danger related to demanding perfection from others exists in all aspects of our lives—at work and at home. In this story, the impossible expectation of perfection was placed on a youth by his parents, and the outcome was devastating. We're all trying to live up to people's expectations, so be kind by setting reasonable, achievable objectives for others. My first career was working with vulnerable populations like people with disabilities, homeless people, those struggling with addiction, and young male sex offenders, but mostly I worked with at-risk youth, and that's when I met James.* James was a 19-year-old who came from an affluent family and was a full-time university student. James' family expected perfection of him, particularly when it came to academic performance, and he felt the pressure. He was facing an exam and feeling a lack of confidence in his ability to do well, and chose to cheat. He was caught. And expelled. When his parents learned of what he'd done, they kicked him out of their home and disowned him. When James found our youth program, he was homeless, scared, hungry, and using drugs. He'd gone from his family home to the streets, with nothing but a backpack. On the street, he quickly learned that he needed to stay awake or risk having his backpack and everything he was, stolen. Crystal meth was his solution. It was a cheap drug that offered lasting results. We did all we could to support James to get on his feet again—engage his mind, clean his body from the drugs, and seek safe housing—but we were too late. The addiction and depression he experienced overtook him, and he chose to end his life. I attended his funeral; his parents did not.

That is a very difficult story for me to write; it still brings me incredible sadness, but you needed to read it because I need you to fully appreciate how unfair, unkind, and inhumane perfection is. It's not OK to expect others to be perfect, and it's not OK to expect yourself to be perfect.

Perfection does not exist. Read that again.

Why do we even strive for perfection—what is the prize? OK, what if I tell you right now that you're perfect? Now what? I spoke to a few perfectionists when writing this chapter and asked them this question; their responses made me chuckle, in a horrific kind of way. They answered by giving me an example to help me understand

---

* Name has been changed to protect his spirit, and his family.

the depth where perfectionism lives. They explained that when they were in school, they wouldn't aim for 100 percent (which I'm sure most of us would agree is a perfect grade), but, rather, strive for the bonus points and earn more than 100 percent. Where does it end? I'm not a perfectionist. In fact, my MBA class mantra was "B's get degrees." Consider this: What do you call a person who finished last in their class in medical school? A doctor.

This makes me wonder: what is the opposite of perfectionism, and whatever it is, is it what perfectionists are trying desperately to avoid? Well, here are a few words that describe the opposite of perfection: ordinary, average, mediocre. Does perfection relate to high achievement? High energy? And the opposite is lazy, apathetic, carefree, careless? I don't have the answer, but from my experience, I've been careless and carefree a lot in my life, and it hasn't been terrible. Sure, I got a few C's in math due to careless mistakes, but my carefree nature has brought me many adventures, and I definitely believe I have a lower level of stress and anxiety than those I know who are striving for perfection. Let's remember that perfection is unattainable; therefore, what we're really talking about is a mindset: how much we are willing to push ourselves to standards that aren't achievable, and that may drain our energy and our self-esteem.

There are limits perfectionism puts on us, many of which can result in debilitating mental health disorders like depression and anxiety. I'm going to focus on one of the limits that many of us have experienced: imposter syndrome. Whether you think you don't deserve to be in your role and are waiting for your peers to realize you don't measure up, or you feel like many of your accomplishments are a result of luck, you have probably had a moment of self-doubt that can be defined as imposter syndrome. Imposter syndrome is a feeling of inadequacy that persists despite all indications that you have earned all you have accomplished. There are three common ways that imposter syndrome shows up, and I've experienced them all. The first is feeling like a fake. Have you ever felt like you are deceiving those around you into believing that you are more competent than you actually are, despite the fact that your knowledge and experience verify that you are competent? Ever thought, "Wait until people find out that I have no idea what I'm doing!"? The expression goes, *Fake it till you make it,* but with imposter syndrome, you're the only one who believes that you're faking it. Most likely, everyone else in the room thinks highly of you.

The second way imposter syndrome shows up is attributing success to luck. I've written a whole chapter ("Bad Words") on this one. This is about thinking that your successes occurred because you were in the right place at the right time, not because you have the capability to achieve that success or because of what you have done. And the third way is discounting success. You are uncomfortable internalizing your successes and instead discount compliments that you receive by saying, "It wasn't important" or "It was an easy win."

Combating imposter syndrome requires comparing you to what your expectation of perfect looks like. Are you comparing yourself to your own expectations? If so, how were those expectations determined? Who or what taught you how to shape those expectations? Are you comparing yourself to others? If so, reread the above paragraphs and remember that others are not perfect either. In fact, they are likely to experience imposter syndrome, too. Seriously, I want you to take a moment and answer these questions. I can't promise you'll never experience imposter syndrome again, but I aim to reduce its frequency by helping you draw a deeper awareness of where it was born in you, what triggers it in you, and how much it limits you. So, answer those questions, and then keep reading.

Perhaps not surprisingly, imposter syndrome was first described in the 1970s by two women in a paper titled "The Imposter Phenomenon in High Achieving Woman: Dynamics and Therapeutic Intervention" (Clance and Imes 1978). Many studies have been conducted on the prevalence of imposter syndrome, and they generally agree that around 75 percent of women have personally experienced it. My experience coaching tells me that number is an underestimate. In fact, it's rare for me to encounter a woman who has not experienced imposter syndrome. Research has also shown that members of minority groups experience a higher occurrence of imposter syndrome, and many straight, Caucasian men also experience it. Message? If you experience imposter syndrome, you're far from alone. Another message? With so many people feeling like they're faking it, can we all agree that no one has it all together? No one is confident all of the time? Final message: In the wise words of my Aunt Joan, be kind to others. Be kind to yourself. Be kind.

Perfection is a catalyst to imposter syndrome, not the cure for it.
I present as very confident, so many assume that I don't suffer from imposter syndrome, but I most certainly do! Let me tell you about a time when I experienced it and when I first learned what it was. I have an undergraduate degree in psychology and worked in non-profit organizations for ten years, so when my boss told me I had a real mind for business and should think about doing an MBA, I literally burst out laughing. Fast forward to a year later, when I thought, "What the heck, I'll apply." Imagine my surprise when I got accepted! Then my first day of school came. I sat in a large room with 91 other students and listened to our professor speak. Suddenly, he stopped and addressed what I can imagine was a room full of overwhelmed adults. He asked, "How many of you feel as though you are

here because we've made some terrible mistake and somehow your application drifted over from the 'no' pile to the 'yes' pile, completely by accident, perhaps due to a breeze blowing in through an open window?" Um, yeah, it was definitely me he was talking about, so I raised my hand. Then he said, "Everyone, look around." I looked around and saw that just about every single person in the room also had their hand up. He said, "Look, we do make the occasional mistake, but we don't make this many of them. You are all here because you deserve to be, and the doubt you are feeling right now is called imposter syndrome."

Want to know another time I've experienced imposter syndrome? While writing this book! I mean, I'm too young and inexperienced to be writing a book—I still have much to learn! Who am I to think my experiences are important enough to hit pages of a book? What makes my lessons and stories special enough that people will actually pay for it? But when those thoughts hit me, I remind myself that we are all always evolving and learning; so if not now, when? And if not me, who? The conditions will never be perfect. I will never be perfect.

I teach this stuff for a living. My mission is to help people feel and radiate confidence, so am I not an imposter if I, myself, suffer from the imposter syndrome? I share this with you because some people might point to me when they think of a strong, confident person. Perhaps to some, I'm their picture of perfection. Telling you about my challenges with this syndrome aims to reinforce once again the fact that no one has it all together; no one feels strong and confident all of the time. We all have our own story, and to assume you know someone else's full story is disrespectful. Most people we think are perfect are people we don't know and whom we've glorified. The reason why it's easier to hold them in such high regard is because we don't know them well. Whereas we know the people closest to us are imperfect: some are always late, some have a short fuse, some struggle with self-care. But in reality (yes, I'm going to say it again), no one is perfect.

We have to stop waiting for perfect conditions. Waiting for the perfect idea to share and then waiting for the perfect time to share it. Too many times I've watched others sit on their ideas because they're not ready yet. They feel more work is needed to perfect the idea, so they keep their idea a big secret while they continue striving for 100 percent perfection, ensuring their idea is fail-proof. Want to know how this ends? Someone else has the same idea and brings it forward when it's 80 percent ready and gets 100 percent of the credit, and you lose out, coming in at a whopping 0 percent. I've worked with thousands of women who complain to me that others steal their ideas or say things that they were thinking. I'll tell you what I tell them. Leadership is having the courage to fail, sharing ideas even though they might not work. And here comes the scariest part: having the courage to be wrong. Ugh. Being wrong sucks.

I work with senior leaders at Fortune 500 companies, and I've asked them how often they get it wrong. Do you know what they say? They usually chuckle and say, *"Brenda, I'm wrong all day! That's all I do. I go from meeting to meeting and am told that I'm wrong, that my idea won't work, but that's my job. I have to be the one who throws spaghetti at the wall and sees what sticks; I have to be the ideas guy. As a leader, I have to take those risks, and my ego has gotten used to being wrong all day."* So, if we want to be seen and heard as leaders, we really need to get more comfortable with getting it wrong. To do so, let's look at why women avoid failure.

There is conflicting research as to whether women are more risk-averse than men, but my experience tells me we definitely are, especially at work. My theory is that women feel they are starting with a deficit, starting behind the starting line, and because of this, we can't afford to trip. In a boardroom full of men, we can't afford to be wrong like men can be. And you know what? This might be true. I mean, we are up against gender biases, but we aren't doing ourselves any favours by keeping our ideas a secret until they are perfect. The truth is that the best ideas and greatest inventions were the result of collaboration (a natural strength we have as women). One person courageously threw spaghetti at a wall; it was not quite ready, it didn't stick, then someone else took that spaghetti, put it in their pot, cooked it a bit more, then threw it at the wall again. This process was repeated until it stuck. Everyone involved gets some credit, and the originator of the idea is seen as a leader simply for bringing their idea forward. Lesson? You don't have to have a fully cooked noodle to win.

The other reason I believe women are more risk-averse is because, generally, we have lower self-esteem and our egos are fragile, which makes the risk of failure very unattractive. Women are waaaaaaaaaay more likely to be perfectionists, and that has us failing a lot. If you're striving for perfection, you're guaranteed to fail, and therein begins the downward spiral of perfection. Ironically, the perfectionist who strives to be the best is always losing. Sadly, although they may be achieving many successes, they never truly feel the pride and joy of those successes. Constantly failing has a significant and negative impact on our confidence. When we repeatedly fail to achieve our goals, we start to doubt ourselves and our ability to succeed. We internalize our "failures" and incorrectly label them as inabilities. Of course, this lack of confidence further limits our appetite for risk. When we are low in confidence, we lose the drive, determination, and energy to try new things, which could result in becoming fearful of meeting new people or engaging in new experiences.

Aside from preventing us from being seen as leaders, risk aversion limits innovation. If you are fearful of trying new things, you are less likely to express new ideas, less likely to suggest new ways of doing things, and, eventually, less creative in your thinking. We know that innovation drives growth, so if we stay within the known safe space and are fearful of trying new things, we will miss out on growth opportunities, growth for ourselves, our families, and our companies.

If you identified with the definition of imposter syndrome or the stories I've shared, please know that, while it is not healthy, it is common, and it doesn't mean you're doomed to feel insecure forevermore. In some circumstances, you may feel one or all of these emotions, but in others, you may be extremely confident in your abilities and experience. And while imposter syndrome contributes to low self-esteem, they are not the same thing. Imposter syndrome can be situational, while low self-esteem tends to linger.

Now that you've given up on perfection and have an understanding of imposter syndrome, I'm going to give you a few ways you can reduce it.

Set yourself up for wins!
Set realistic, attainable goals and celebrate your successes. Success breeds success, so create favourable conditions for yourself. Here's an example: Let's say you have a goal of running a half-marathon. You wake up one Sunday morning and say, "This is it! Today's the day I run the half," but 20 minutes into the run, your legs are tired and you're running out of steam. You decide to stop and walk the rest of the way home. Feeling defeated, you begin saying unkind things to yourself like, "See, I told you you're not a runner" and "Nice try, loser." What are the odds you're going to lace up again tomorrow and

try again? Low. Quite low. Now imagine this: same goal, more realistic expectations of your Sunday run. You wake up Sunday morning and say, "This is it! Today's the day I begin my training for the half!" You set an achievable goal of running for 20 minutes, with two optional walking minutes if you need them. After running for 20 minutes, you're back at your door. Feeling accomplished, you make a healthy lunch, call your friend to flaunt your success, and plan the rest of the week's runs. What are the odds you're going to lace up again tomorrow and try again? High. Quite high.

Make a flaunt file.
When you're feeling like you haven't accomplished anything valuable and you don't belong in your role, having a file of positive feedback (emails, letters, reviews, etc.) that you have received is a great way to revisit your successes. This is tangible proof that you do provide value. Another tip: be sure to share your flaunt file, or pieces of it, often! When I'd receive positive comments from clients or testimonies from course participants, I'd always (yes, always) forward them to my boss. I did it so often that eventually I made a joke of it and would put "another satisfied customer" in the subject line of my emails. My boss got a kick out of me, but you know what else he got? Valuable insight into my wins.

Do your best to not compare yourself to others.
Often times, self-doubt comes from comparing yourself to someone who you feel has accomplished major successes. First of all, it is not useful to compare yourself to others. Everyone operates in a different manner and grows at his or her own pace. Secondly, remember that everyone has moments of self-doubt. Even those people who you look up to have moments where they feel like an imposter.

Remember that being wrong doesn't make you a fake.
People make mistakes. Mistakes are what help people learn and grow, even if it is hard to hear that you are wrong. I know I remember and learn from my mistakes way more than I remember and learn from my wins. I can tell you that my biggest mistake when I was starting out in my career was that I'd received and accepted a verbal agreement on a price rather than requiring it in writing. The quoted price changed later in the project, and I was at fault. This was a very costly mistake to my company, but let me tell you, I've never done that again. Being wrong does not make you a fake; it means you are taking chances and looking for opportunities to take risks and innovate.

Get comfortable saying "I don't know."
Some of the most intelligent people are the ones who are comfortable saying, "I don't know." They are smart enough to acknowledge that they don't know the answer and are confident enough to say that they are unsure of the solution. Not knowing the answer does not make you a fraud.

Regularly update your resume.
Updating your resume is a great opportunity to review your growth and acknowledge your recent accomplishments while reflecting on your early achievements. Incorporating new skills and experiences will help your resume and your confidence!

Don't argue with your champions.
When other people see potential in you, accept it. If leaders say they think you're ready for a promotion, don't argue with them, even if you don't believe it yourself. Remember that our tendency is to be overly self-critical, while others see us in a more honest way. In the

same vein, when someone gives you a compliment, don't swat it away; it's a gift! Accept it with grace. Finally, give attention to what's truly being said, not what your mind wants to focus on. If I say you're awesome, you're awesome, you're awesome, you're awesome, you're awesome, you suck, you're awesome. What do you remember? Right, so ... stop doing *that*.

Here's what I want for you: I want you to embrace your imperfection and see it as human. Instead of perfection, strive towards doing your best. Remember: the only thing we are all perfect at is being imperfect. So, aim to be perfect at being you—the good and bad. Doing so will reduce your fears and anxiety and boost your confidence.

CHAPTER 3

Bad Words

I just think I'm lucky. I get to write this cool book for you, and I hope it helps you in some way. I'm pretty sure it will.

Yuck. That was hard for me to write. Um, wait … you knew I was kidding, making a point, right? Oh my. Here's the deal: We talk like this so much that it may not have sounded weird to you as you read it. Well, here we are, and this is the very reason for this chapter. If I had to capture the message of this chapter in a word, I'd say it's about **ownership**.

The main issue I have with these words is not only the language but what they do to our mindset. Remember from the previous chapter that what we say to ourselves is powerful. Our brains are not only crafting the words we use, but they are also listening to them. Our brains are the authors *and* the audience of our communication. Language is a telling signal about our ideas and our confidence of them. In that sense, the last sentence said informs the confidence with which we deliver the next.

We are so quick to own our failures, our weaknesses, or shortcomings—even when others were involved. But when given the same degree of ownership, responsibility, and accountability for our wins, we become fearful. Don't be afraid of the power of ownership. *Don't shy away from winning.* Embrace the whole process—from setting the goal to going the distance to crossing the finish line. It may feel unnatural at first to give yourself credit for everything you do, but do yourself a huge favour and get used to it.

Here are the words I dislike: *luck, hope, should, but, think, just, never,* and *always.* Effective immediately, I want you to consider these to be bad words. Generally, bad words are words to be used seldomly, cautiously, and with select audiences. These same rules apply to my bad words. For example, use the word "think" only when you are actually thinking about something.

How did I come to dislike these words so much? I'll tackle this one word at a time.

LUCK

I'm not sure if I've mentioned this yet or not, but I'm kind of a big deal. I've had some success in my career—climbed the corporate ladder, travelled extensively, worked with impressive executives—and so, yeah, I'm a big deal. Naturally, I am often approached by young, keen professionals, who want to know how I did it. Sometimes I want to say, "A bowl of raisin bran every morning, a bowl of berries every night," to be funny. Really, there is no formula. We all have our own path. I love listening to their questions because I learn so much. I learn what matters to them, the thought processes of aspiring youth, and how I can stay relevant to others. They really make me think. It was one of these junior associates that made me realize how much I recoil when I hear the word *luck*.

One morning, a young intern, new to our firm, met me in the hallway outside our office. She was smart; she had been paying attention, and she had a question for me. At 7:20 a.m. on a Monday morning, in the hallway, before I'd even entered the office, she had a question for me. She asked me how much of my success I attribute to luck. Wow, good question. A stumper. I had to buy myself some time. This is unusual for me; I'm usually quite quick on my feet and full of answers, but I felt the weight of this question. I still do; it's now in a book 10 years later. I bought myself until the end of the day and told her I'd get back to her. After thinking about it, here's how I responded: I told her I was *lucky* for the socio-economic conditions in which I was born. *Lucky* for parents who loved me and did their best to raise me with good values and ethics. Aside from that, nothing. I filled with pride as I said every sentence in an increasingly louder voice. I earned the rest. I worked hard for my success. But I didn't always feel this way.

When I was in my twenties, I remember coining the phrase "Lucky Landry." I really believed that we Landrys were luckier than the rest of the world, because it didn't feel difficult or like hard work to get to where I was, and I was so happy with my life. I figured that it must be the case that I and our family were just lucky. We grew up in a lower-middle-class family, ate chicken out of a can, lived in rented houses, and moved around in leased cars. My father was in insurance sales, and we rode the rollercoaster of variable income, pivoting from eating Kraft Dinner three nights a week to having three cars in the driveway (with only two drivers living there). Regardless of what was happening in Dad's bank account, we were always up. We lived a consistently good life despite inconsistent circumstances. His attitude sheltered us to some degree, and this led to me believing that we were a lucky family. Now I know that underneath almost all good luck stories lies turbulence, hard work, wins, failures, and a few spurts of bad luck.

Back to my intern's question. She'd made me reflect, and when I did, I discovered that I did work hard for what I had achieved. So how does this reconcile with the "Lucky Landry" theory? Well, I enjoyed what I was doing so much that it didn't feel like hard effort or work. But it *was* work. All I had achieved required me to make courageous decisions, take action, be uncomfortable with risks, try, fail, and sometimes win. It was concentrated, intentional effort. I worked for it, I deserved it, and today I own it. I own my successes. Allow me to use this opportunity to flaunt.

I had a super cool job as a lifeguard when I was a teenager. This gave me some extra cash, and connections with the coolest kids in town. But I wasn't *lucky* to get that job. I was at the pool from 6 a.m. to 9 p.m., more days than not. I successfully completed all the courses and exams needed to qualify as a lifeguard. My blonde hair was green. I worked 30 hours a week while going to university full time, and I was legally responsible for people's lives. It was years of dedication, passion, and drive that helped me get that super cool lifeguard job. Nothing about this was luck.

I had a fulfilling job managing an employment program for at-risk youth in Vancouver, B.C. That wasn't luck, either. I earned a psychology degree and landed jobs supporting some of society's most vulnerable populations. I worked with adults with rage disorders, young male sex offenders, children with autism, and homeless addicts. It was years of learning and connecting that helped me get that cool management job. Nothing about this was luck.

Today, I have a well-established reputation as an executive consultant. Still, no luck at play here. I put myself back to school when I was 33 years old to get my MBA. I had to learn things like corporate finance, contract law, and business research. I put myself $60,000 in debt. It was years of courage and ambition that led me to this—my current job. Nothing about this was luck.

I'm sure this was a longer answer than my intern was looking for, but, hey, I had to make my point.

Now, a good writer always considers the opposing view, and really, the story above is my story. So let me broaden my message by acknowledging that your upbringing, environment, and health can definitely impact your starting point in life. And some of you may feel very unlucky. That said, I do truly believe that your mindset can be the middle and end of your journey.

Determination, resilience, and positivity are the keys to creating the life you want, regardless of where your story began. In fact, even in my own family, there are differences in our confidence and appetite for risk. My older sister picked up on different cues from our upbringing, which resulted in an adult life of living with anxiety and some rooted insecurities. For this reason, many would say that my sister was less *lucky*. Not me; read on. Our mother was a nervous, anxious woman who always questioned, "What if…?" and, as usual, my sister was paying more attention than I. My sister was an introverted, highly intelligent child and placed tremendous value on her academic performance, so when she was made fun of in school, it translated to a fear of public speaking later in life. Despite these stark differences in how we experienced childhood, today we are both confident women leaders in our field; she just had to work harder to get there. And that's my point. She, like many, could have accepted that these experiences were going to limit her to a life of insecurity and living from a place of fear. Instead, she worked hard to overcome her well-founded anxiety, rather than use it as a convenient reason to remain blocked. How? She courageously worked with a therapist, "Larry," who challenged her cognitive constructs and empowered her to tap into the bravery that lived in her. It was inspiring to witness. For all of you reading this, get some therapy. We can all improve.

Message: *The bits and pieces of your life that informed your insecu-*

rities can be released; you can choose to move beyond them. *You can choose to be and do more; it's in you to do so.*

We can all alter our reality; it's a life choice, and you (only you) have the power to do it. Someone once told me that our lives are like a book with a beginning, middle, and end, with many chapters along the way. One or more event or sequence of experiences makes up a chapter. My sister literally rewrote the middle and end chapters of her life. I, too, had been in really terrible situations that could have derailed me forever. Instead, like my sister, I categorized them as a chapter in my book—not the full story of who I am. Some of you may be carrying scars that run deep and will take more than positive outlook to heal, and I get that. However, I encourage you to not use excuses of poor circumstances for how your life turns out. It is all too common that people create a self-fulfilling prophecy of only rising to the limits that were established in childhood. Don't fall into this trap. Raise your own bar. Take control. Own your reality.

The danger in overusing the word *luck* is that it can detract from the role you played in making something happen. Here are a few everyday examples of misusing this word.

My friend gets invited to another friend's cottage. I say, "Oh, wow! You're so lucky!" Is she? Is that luck? Or is it that she has earned a reputation as someone people like to spend time with, developed a strong friendship, and possibly is a fun source of entertainment?

Here's another. My friends and I get seated at the best table on a restaurant patio. Amazing! How lucky! Sun and an umbrella, sitting next to flowers, it's the prime spot. Was that luck? It could be a bit of luck; it could be timing; but it also could very well be that my group looks like a lot of fun, and the host has decided that our energy will boost the experience of their other guests. Since it could be any one, or a combination of those reasons, I say it's wrong to chalk that up to luck.

Why are we so quick to label wins as luck? Luck is the opposite of ownership, and since we're working on recognizing and celebrating our successes, I encourage you to challenge yourself when you're attributing something you or someone else did to luck. Dig deep, in most cases, you'll find that a decision made, or an action you did, is behind all of this miraculous luck that you and others seem to be discovering.

Let's keep *luck* a word we only use when something happens to us or others that we truly had no hand in creating, like finding a twenty-dollar bill on the street.

HOPE

Most people in my life would say I am an incredibly positive person who walks through the world with a high degree of optimism, so why do I consider *hope* to be a bad word? Isn't hopefulness synonymous with optimism? Great question, Brenda. The answer brings us back to the theme of this chapter: ownership.

You can be hopeful, so long as you remember that hope will only get you so far. Hope doesn't imply will, means, or intent. You cannot just wish away your problems, hope for change, or dream about your future. You need to act to change your situation.

By now, I'm sure you're getting this message loud and clear—it's up to you! I can appreciate that this can feel overwhelming. If you want something, you need to act. There is no one who can own this for you or do this for you; you are fully accountable. But I *hope* (kidding ;)) that you also feel empowered by this. You don't have to do it alone. In most instances, having support is not only helpful but needed. Ultimately, though, you are the centre of it all, the eye of the storm that will stir up the present and create the future you want. There is no magic button, or Prince Charming, or special fad diet, or lottery winnings that are miraculously going to come into your life and solve your problems. When you really want something, you must move beyond hope. Real ownership creates real change.

You may have heard the saying, "Hope is not a strategy." That's because strategy is just a fancy word for a plan, whereas hope is passive. Hope can be the starting point for a dream, and dreams can be the starting point for a goal. Goals can then be broken into a plan that then requires action to make the change. But that's it. Hope alone will accomplish nothing. For real change, you've got to make it fucking happen.

Let's test a couple of hopes:

I *hope* I get to travel to Italy this year.

I *hope* people living homeless have enough to eat.

Clearly, simply hoping these things will not change any realities. True story, I had a childhood dream to visit Italy. I have no idea where my obsession with this country came from, but it was very real. By the time I hit 40, I'd travelled to over 25 countries, and still hadn't been to Italy! Hoping to get there wasn't working. I didn't get lucky (see what I did there), hope didn't make an airplane ticket arrive in my inbox. I'll tell you what did, me! I decided I was going. With or without friends. I did tell a few people I was planning to go in September, and they could join if they wanted, but I was going. My days of hoping to get there were over; hope turned into a plan, and yes, I went to Italy. Damn straight.

As for improving the lives of the homeless, let me assure you, your hopes do not fill their tummies.

Turn your hopes into actions and watch your life change.

The language we use tells people how to take what we're saying. When we speak with weak language, we tell others not to place too much value on what we're saying. When we speak with certainty, we tell others to have confidence in our ideas. The biggest offenders of minimizing the power of your message are *just* and *think*.

Here are some examples:

"I was *just thinking* that maybe we should..." Count the tentative words in that sentence. Did you find four? If not, try again. *Just, think, maybe,* and *should*. How would you rewrite this? Here's my suggestion: replace it all with "Let's."

"I *just* have a little bit of an idea." If someone said that to you, how excited would you be to hear what comes next? For most, it would be a signal to stop listening. Instead, say, "I have an idea," or, even better, "I have a great idea!"

Let's look at these words one at a time.

JUST

I feel like it would be most appropriate if the word *just* could be made smaller. Abbreviated somehow. Maybe "Jst" or "J't." It is, quite intentionally, a minimizing word. Its job is to detract from the significance of what comes after it. "I *just* need five minutes"—here, we're attempting to make five minutes seem less than what it is, which is five minutes. *Just* can also be used as an indication of a small amount of time, meaning recently—I *just* finished working out. Here, we're not trying to minimize working out; we're simply saying it happened not long ago. This is an appropriate use of the word. It's the minimizing use of the word that makes it a bad word.

Use it knowing what it does, which is to make what follows it seem insignificant. I said earlier that bad words are words to be used seldomly, cautiously, and with select audiences, and that we must use these words with intention. With *just*, be sure to not use it when it is not appropriate to make what comes next seem small. Here are examples of how it can be well used and poorly used.

Well used: "I *just* [meaning recently] got off the phone with Eva."

Poorly used: "I *just* [meaning only] wrote the report; Alycia did all of the research."

THINK

I can almost promise that every single person reading this right now overuses the word *think*. Why do people use the word *think* so much? I have two theories. First, it's a risk mitigation strategy. It intentionally lessens the certainty and ownership of your thought or idea. If your idea is wrong, or not well-received, it can protect you because you were only *thinking* it. But here's the deal with risk mitigation: low risk, low reward, which means if your idea was a good one, you equally don't get to own the win because you were only *thinking* it. My second theory is that it's become a language habit, a bad language habit.

I misused the word *think* once at work and got schooled very quickly. One day, I walked into my boss's office and started out by saying, "Hey, I think we should..." I was quickly cut off and told, "So, Brenda, we have this really nice office for you down the hall, and that's where we pay you to do your thinking. When you come here, I need you to know." I laughed uncomfortably. He wasn't joking. Then I said, "Oh, well, I know, I do know!" He replied, "Then say that." After that, I realized that I, and so many others I know, overuse the word *think*. I know, sometimes we really are still thinking; we have an idea, it's not fully formed, and we're looking to brainstorm. In those cases, *think* is an appropriate word. All other times, it's not. Remember, we can use this and other bad words when it's appropriate. Use the word *think* only when you're actually still in contemplation.

BUT and SHOULD

As I mentioned, my first career was working in non-profit organizations. Not the big ones, the little grassroots ones who had about $500 a year to spend on office supplies for 15 staff and 150 clients. All of this is to say, money was tight. So, when I attended a conference and learned that they had hired a speaker who was being paid $5,000, I paid close attention to her every word. After all, she must be about to share some very important stuff at that price tag! She was from a very affluent neighbourhood in Vancouver; she was wearing a head-to-toe red leather outfit, and she exuded presence. I listened closely and was somewhat disappointed when gold wasn't tossed into the air at some point. I did take away two powerful lessons, which I will share with you now, as I have with so many before, so that I could extend the reach of her message and squeeze every single bit of value out of that little non-profit spend. Here's what I learned: Don't use the words *but* or *should*.

Let's look at the function of the word *but*, by looking at what it does to a sentence. "I like your shoes, but your dress is not a nice colour." What would your response be? I'll tell you, most would say, "What's wrong with this colour?!" Here's another one: "You are doing a great job with our customers, but you need to be stronger at managing your files." Again, all of our focus goes to the part of the sentence that comes after the word *but*. If this is so, why even say the first part of the sentence? Some might say the front part is a buffer; it softens the blow. This is flawed logic, since we know that we don't even hear the front part of the sentence. It's not softening the blow; it's entirely unnecessary, and it can even be condescending or insulting.

Now, let's look at *should*. You really should stop using the word *should*. It doesn't imply will, means, or intent. In fact, I'd say it's anchored in guilt, which is a useless emotion. It can also point to obligation, which is not where we find joy. Instead, consider using *could* or *will*.

Let's test it.

"I really *should* go to the gym today." What does this mean? Am I going to go? Who knows! All we know is that I feel like it's the right thing to do; it doesn't mean I'm planning to go or will go.

How about this, instead:

"I *could* go to the gym today." Here, I'm pointing out that I see it as an option, and if I decide to go, I'll make a plan. Or, "I *will* go to the gym today."

If you're not comfortable saying either *could* or *will*, drop your sense of obligation and feelings of guilt and rethink that activity.

Bottom line: You shouldn't *should* all over yourself, and you shouldn't *should* all over others, either.

NEVER and ALWAYS

Extreme certainty doesn't exist. Nothing is *always* something, or *never* something. How would you react if I were to say to you that you *never* call me? I can guess you'd react defensively. What if I said you *always* blame me for not being on time. The problem with both of these words is that they are too easy to argue. I *never* call you? What about that time when... I *always* blame you? What about that time when... They are generally argumentative words that will create adverse reactions, which are likely to escalate a situation, not diffuse it.

Other words that have no place in your mouth

Many of us use what are called filler words. They are called that because they are literally filling the air, the space, the silence. The most common filler words are "um" and "ah." Why do we feel we need to fill silence? There are two reasons: one, we're trying to avoid interruption, trying to keep the floor and not lose our turn to talk, so we just keep talking and talking, and when there aren't real words available, we insert filler words. What is so wrong with being interrupted? Who cares if someone steals the floor by interjecting their ideas on the topic? Likely, what's wrong is, we are insecure in our ability to get the floor back. Instead of seeing interruption as a bad thing, see it as a sign that your audience is interested and engaged in your topic. Also, when you speak with confidence, interruptions will lessen. (More on this in the *"You, Out Loud"* chapter.) The second reason is that it's become a language habit, a bad language habit. Get over your fear of silence and use a pause to let your next word come to you.

Next, let's look at a category I call validating words, OK?

I'd like your permission, you know?

It's important to state ideas with confidence, right?

I'd be more comfortable if you came right out and said, "I'm feeling insecure; please assure me that I'm doing OK." I coached a very successful executive woman who used to say, *"You know?"* after almost every sentence. She otherwise presented as very confident, so I was determined to help her overcome this habit. We started by looking at where it came from. It seems the root was that English is her second language, and she was used to seeking validation to ensure her audience was understanding her. However, that need was outdated. Her English was now perfect, yet the language habit had remained and was not serving her well. I had her in a group training session, so I recruited the rest of the participants to help increase her awareness of the frequency in which she uses the phrase. I asked the class that every time they hear her say, *"You know?"* to respond, out loud, "No, we don't know. Please keep telling us." And the number of times they had to interrupt her talk was real-time feedback for her, showing her how often she was using the phrase. The increased awareness helped, and with focused practice, she was able to eliminate using it.

There is another category we need to talk about, and that's bad starter words. It's OK to use the words *and* and *so* to begin sentences once in a while; generally, however, it is a poor disguise for a run-on sentence. They are also another strategy people use to decrease the chance they will be interrupted. If I just keep on talking, with grammar that sounds like one very long sentence, people will be less likely to interrupt me, since people tend to interrupt during pauses, at the end of a thought or sentence, not partway through it. Like what I said about filler words, this strategy doesn't work and reeks of insecurity. Sure, people might interrupt you less, but they've also stopped listening and likely have lost confidence in you. I like to say, "Let the audience hear the punctuation." Meaning, when you get to the end of the sentence, stop and pause. This is most effective when the next sentence begins as a new thought, not a continuation of the one before it. In the chapter "You, Out Loud," you'll learn more about the power of the pause.

The next category is best referred to as bullshit words, and while there is only one word here, *like*, it deserves its own category. I was *like* going to put this one first, but *like* I knew you'd be expecting it. I *like* asked my friend if she *like* thinks it's a misused word, and she *like* totally agreed that I should *like* talk about it in here. Research tells us that the misuse of this word originates in California teen and valley girl culture. Overuse of the word will commonly assign you with brand attributes such as stupidity or an airhead personality. While these labels can be overcome by projecting intelligence and confidence in other ways, the biggest issue I have with it is that it completely turns an audience off. Many people have told me that when they hear *like* used as every second word, it's all they can hear.

This means they miss out on the substance you have and the ideas you are trying to share.

Mostly, we're using *like* as meaning "similar to," but how often does someone need to note similarity to something rather than just being that something? Its misuse is tentative, weak, and insecure—all words you don't want associated with your brand. More on your leadership brand in the chapter, "Flaunt Your Face Off." For now, let's all agree that using definite statements with bold confident language is the way to go.

How to stop using these words
It is possible to eliminate the bad words we've covered in this chapter, and doing so will help you to appear (and feel) more confident. It's worth it. We tend to spend a lot of time making sure we look good—polished appearance, perfect PowerPoint slides—yet we undermine it all through using language that tells our audience that we don't even believe in what we're saying.

Know that you have the ability to control the words you say. I remember when I was in grade three and I discovered swearing. Yes, grade three. I swore at school with my friends. A lot. Then it struck me, while sitting on the toilet at home one day, "Oh my God, what if I can't turn it off?" If I swear like that at home, I'll get in shit! Panic set in; I didn't know if it was possible to use certain language with some crowds, and not with others. I reassured myself by thinking that adults must do this all the time. I'm sure teachers swear, yet somehow, they turn it off when they are teaching us all day. So, yes, it had to be possible. I'm proud to say it was years later before my dad picked up the phone at the wrong time and heard his "angel" using very colourful language.

For many, these are language habits, and like all habits, they take time to break. Like all change, it'll take attention and intention to make the change. Step-by-step, here's how to do it.

Increase your self-awareness.
- **Reread the last 20 emails you sent.** Are you ready to see how often you use bad words and what your biggest offenders are? Read your sent emails. They are tangible evidence of your language habits. Find the bad words and rewrite every sentence using stronger, more confident language (see next chapter, "Good Words"). If appropriate, resend the email!
- **Record yourself and listen back.** We're often better behaved, more diligent with our use of language when we write. That's why the words you found yourself using in step one are likely the tip of the iceberg. It's time to dial into our audio tracks. If you have access to a second device, record your side of the conversation. Perhaps you're on a Zoom call. Record using your mobile phone. If you're on your phone, use your computer, another phone, or a tablet to record you speaking. Listen back multiple times. Write out every sentence you say using a bad word, and then rewrite the sentence using stronger, more confident language.
- **Recruit a trusted friend or co-worker.** Ask someone who is with you often to signal to you when you're using bad words. Help them by telling them what you learned about your habits through completing the first two steps above. If *like* is your biggest offender, ask them to point out when you're using that word. Note: You may (likely) have more than one bad word you'd like to stop using; I'd suggest you begin with the most frequently used one. Isolate it, focus on it, and when that habit is broken, move on to the next word.

Practice real-time correction.
- **Be diligent in writing.** When we improve how we communicate in writing, it translates to speaking. That's why you need to reread everything you write multiple times before sharing it with others. In the same way that you might edit your writing for grammar or punctuation, now you must do the same for usage of bad words. Literally edit these words out of your vocabulary.
- **Drive yourself crazy.** As you begin hearing yourself saying bad words, it will drive you crazy. I promise. That's exactly what we want. It will become like hearing nails on a chalkboard. That creates a mental discomfort known as cognitive dissonance, and it will prompt your brain to correct for it.
- **Slow down.** Let your brain catch up with that mouth of yours! Rather than going on autopilot, go back into that big brain of yours and dig deeper into the vocabulary you have. I think about it as a file folder. When we're speaking quickly, our brain only has time to access the primary files, pulling from the words we use every day—the common words we are trying to eliminate. Instead, slow down the pace of your talking and give yourself time to reach further back, access better words. You'll be amazed with what your brain grabs for you! This is one reason why we tend to do better in writing; we are more intentional; we take the time. Our fingers can't go as fast as our mouth.
- **Correct yourself out loud.** Have you ever heard someone say, "I think ... wait, no ... I KNOW"? If so, they've probably read this book. Correcting yourself out loud does two things: it reminds your brain that you don't use that bad word anymore, and it shares the learning with others. You're affirming your confidence out loud, and that will impress and inspire people. It's not

a weakness; it's strength, and it makes me smile every time I hear someone do it.

You may feel that eliminating these words will leave your communication coming across as too strong and blunt. To that I say, there are other ways you can personalize your communication and show empathy, other than weakening your message and minimizing your ideas. Remember, all other words are still available to you!

Bad words are negatively impacting the confidence we have in ourselves and that others have in us. Don't shy away from winning. Own your power. The objective is to feel and flaunt your best self, and the words we use are an essential ingredient.

Note to readers: Read this entire chapter again before proceeding to the next chapter, "Good Words."

CHAPTER 4

Good Words

After reading that last chapter, you're probably wondering: what *can* you say? After all, I likely stripped you of the top words you use most frequently in a day. Not to worry! I have some new words, stronger words, that you can use in their place. These words, good words, will help you to be taken seriously, be heard, and be perceived for what you are: a strong, confident person.

Words matter. The language you use tells someone what to think of you and what you're saying. When people listen to you speak, they are gathering bits of information that collectively form their opinion of you in that moment and beyond. Believe it or not, the words you use are so important that they can override even the most confident body language, strongest voice, and polished poise. Imagine this: You're sitting around a table waiting for a meeting to begin, and the leader walks in. Let's call him Alex. Alex looks great. Great suit, beaming smile, confident posture, and looks ready to take on the world. Everyone sits and waits for Alex to speak. When he does, he opens with this message: "We have a lot of work to do, and I'm not sure we can get through it all, but we have to try. The Board has placed a great deal of pressure on me and on us, so we really mustn't fail. Now, let's get to work!" How would you feel after hearing Alex's opening remarks? Inspired? Pumped up? Encouraged? Likely not. How about anxious? Pessimistic? Nervous? Trepidatious? Now, consider this: if you're feeling this way, and likely others are, too, what will be the outcome of that meeting? Will you have achieved your objectives? I'll answer this one: it's unlikely. Why? Alex's language set you up for failure before you even began.

Let's look at the words that got in his way. "I'm not sure." Well, Alex, if you're not sure, then I'm not sure! Confidence is contagious, and so is the lack of it. "We have to try." Try is all you want? Ok, Alex, I'll *try*. You haven't asked for my best work; you haven't recruited my enthusiasm; you haven't inspired determination, so I'll just try. "Pressure." The moment that word came out of Alex's mouth, everyone in the room felt it, and while some say they work best under pressure (myself included), we all do so under a strained degree of anxiety and stress, neither of which are conditions for group accomplishment. "We mustn't fail." Oh, my. No room for failure here; there goes my courage for sharing creative or innovative ideas.

OK, same meeting, but Alex has been replaced by Ashley, and Ashley opens the meeting like this: "I'm so glad you're all here. We have a lot of work to do, and I'm confident that by working together, we will get through it all. This work is meaningful to the Board, and I know they will be pleased with our result. Now, let's get to work!" How would you feel after hearing Ashley's opening remarks? Encouraged? Motivated? Excited? Yeah, me too. Words matter.

It's important to notice that the work at hand didn't change, and the pressure didn't lessen. What changed was the language the leader used to introduce the meeting objective. There will be times when you feel uncertain and nervous, and those feelings are valid; however, remember that people will focus on what you tell them to focus on. I like to use a downhill skiing analogy when explaining this (despite the fact, or perhaps because of the fact, that I am a terrible skier). Here's what I know about skiing: if you look at the trees, focus on the trees, and repeatedly tell yourself not to end up in the trees, you quite likely will end up wrapped around the trees. Our mind (and self-talk) tells our body what to do. In this case, trees, pay attention to those trees! Our eyes focus on them, then our head follows. Next, our entire body is facing them, including our legs that have skis attached to them. Instead, point people in the direction you want them to focus. The words we say to ourselves was a focus of the first chapter; now we're seeing that the words we say to others matter equally as much.

In chapter three, "Bad Words," hopefully (I'm kidding!) you gathered that there are words that weaken your message by diminishing the power of what you are saying. In this chapter, you will see that there are words that have an equal, yet opposite, impact; they add to the power of your message.

Now, before we get into my favourite words, I will say that some of you may find these words *too strong*. So strong, in fact, that today you might not be using them often, if at all. I encourage you to begin incorporating them into your vocabulary. Try them out in low-risk situations, like conversations with people you feel safe around. See how it feels using them on a call with your friend, in a meeting with a trusted peer, or while having dinner with your partner. Using strong, bold, confident language will create good outcomes for you. You'll be taken more seriously, you'll be heard, interrupted less, seen as a leader, and valued. Words matter.

Now, let's dive into them.

CONFIDENT

It only makes sense that we start with the word confident. The brand qualities that are attributed to us are often assigned through language. People often describe me as confident, and while I am a confident woman, the fact that I use the word confident so much when I speak certainly doesn't hurt. You'll read more about how to create your own desired leadership brand in the final chapter, "Flaunt Your Face Off."

It's been mentioned before, but it's worth repeating: the words you use when talking about yourself or your ideas are not only telling others what to think about you, but are also offering what's called neurofeedback to your own brain, telling it what to think and believe about yourself. That's why using the word confident is win-win.

I can choose to say, "I think you'll learn something new in this chapter," or I can say, "I am confident that you'll learn something new in this chapter." Does saying I'm confident mean I'm perfect? That I know it all? That I can't possibly be wrong? Not at all. Confidence is not the same as arrogance because of the presence of humility. I can say that I'm confident *and* be proven wrong. That neither lessens my confidence nor makes me a fake. When I say that I'm confident that you're going to learn something new, I am basing this assertion on my general idea of who you are as a reader. I certainly could be wrong. Perhaps you're a linguistics expert who knows way more about this topic than I do. Perhaps you've taken a course in this area or otherwise had prior learning. Should either of these two realities be true, I'd be wrong. But based on the information I have today about the average demographic make-up of this book's audience, I am confident that new learning will be achieved. Perhaps it already has. What I'm doing when I say I'm confident is speaking confidently about that which I know. Unknowns are unknowns and therefore do not need to be accounted for in every sentence that you deliver. There's no need to confess to every potential unknown variable that may exist before you say your point. These disclaimers were debunked in the chapter on bad words. You'll remember from chapter two that none of us are perfect, and none of us know it all. With that as a net neutralizer, let's get more comfortable describing ourselves and our ideas with confidence.

CONVINCED

I often train leaders to speak with conviction, because that degree of certainty is what's needed to engage and excite people, generate aligned thinking, and inspire action. Leaders will say to me, "Yes, that's what I want! How do I do that?" I tell them to use the word *convinced*. Imagine you and I are on a road trip—you're driving, and I'm the navigator. We're lost. I look at a map and report back, "I'm convinced the next exit is the one we need." Do you question me? Likely not. Alternatively, if I said, "Well, it looks like there are a few options; it's kind of hard to tell, but I think this next exit is the one we want." What would you do? I'd guess you'd pull over and review the map yourself. Rightly so. I've done nothing to inspire your trust or confidence.

I worked with a CFO in the energy sector who had to speak to a room full of investment analysts and answer questions about his company's ability to maintain value to its shareholders despite declining commodity prices. His response was this: "We are pretty sure we will be able to weather the storm." Moments later, the stock price of that company plummeted. Not a coincidence. Dude, if you're only *pretty sure*, I'm pulling my money out of your company. This is the clearest, most real-life example I can offer to show you the impact confident language can have on our lives and businesses. When he and I watched the footage of that Q&A and he heard his response, he grimaced. Even he felt the confidence of the market fall. We worked on reframing that response for future use. Here's what we came up with: "We are convinced we have the leadership, assets, and people needed to get through this market challenge."

KNOW

Look, when you know, you know! This is the word I'd like you to use in place of the bad word, *think*. People I coach often say they want to come across as knowledgeable in their field, but they are hesitant to use the word *know*. Due to the rate of industrial progress, innovation is at the center of every company's strategy. Innovation simply means new ideas. That's why we're now in what's called a knowledge-based economy. Your knowledge and your ideas are worth something, and people want to hear them! To help others compartmentalize properly, label your ideas as knowledge rather than thoughts. Get comfortable owning your knowledge. When you know, you know.

I'm absolutely amazing at...

This book is all about remembering our value, noticing our wins, feeling proud of ourselves, and sharing our successes out loud. Collectively, this is called *flaunting*. As you've read elsewhere in this book, you flaunting is good for you and others. There's an entire chapter waiting for you at the end of this book called "Flaunt Your Face Off," which will talk more about self-promotion. For now, here's what you need to know. Labelling your self-promotion as flaunts, wins, or successes, is letting others know that you are proud of what you've done or can do and that you're confident enough to toot your own horn. Let me show you how it sounds.

Imagine your boss is about to assign someone on your team the responsibility of supervising the summer interns. You see this as a leadership opportunity and are keen to do it. There are a few steps that all need to happen to win this assignment. First step: you need to see yourself as worthy. Do you genuinely believe that you have what it takes to lead these students? You have to feel it to flaunt it. Second step: put your hand up. Don't wait for someone to pick you out of the crowd; raise your hand high and with confidence. Third step: you have to be compelling in your pitch for the job. This is where flaunting comes in. Beyond just indicating that you're interested, you need to sell yourself. Go back to step one, assuming you do believe that you have what it takes to do this work; remind yourself what convinced you of that, then package it in an audience-centered way. My guess is that you have a lot you can choose from when picking what to flaunt. Make sure your flaunt is something your boss is going to care about. Perhaps you'll remind them of a recent win you had that they were really excited about. When communicating your value, you need to ensure that what you are saying can be substantiated with real, relevant examples. This relates to the authenticity of your self-promotion—if what you are saying is not true or cannot be proven, people are not going to believe it. Basically, don't make shit up. Ok, here's how it sounds: "Andrew, I'm very interested in the supervisor opportunity, and I'm confident I'm the best person to do it. Here's why. You may recall that I exceeded your expectations with onboarding our new recruits last fall. The feedback from the orientations was clear evidence that I created a welcoming environment, which got others excited about working with us. I bring the energy and organization it takes to create a positive entrance into our organization. These are leadership skills that I'll draw from with our new summer interns."

Read my message to Andrew again. Can you imagine yourself

saying something like that? Does it feel weird to say? If it feels awkward to you, read it again and again. This is the language that works.

"I"

The way I see it, we need to use these good words more often.
The one thing I want you to know is that using these words are powerful—to you and others.

What do you notice about the two sentences above? Well, they both have the word "I" in them. Have the courage and confidence to attribute what you're saying to you! If you're noticing a bit of a theme here—ownership—then I'm doing my job well. You might also notice, particularly in the second sentence, that I've written it with great clarity and certainty. Direct your audience's attention to the one point you want them to focus on. Why one? I'll explain through an example. How good are you at throwing one tennis ball in the air? Pretty good, I bet. How about two? Can you juggle two? Honestly, I'd already be dropping balls here. OK, what about three, four, five? There's a reason that jugglers are so fun to watch, and it's because it's something most of us can't do. Same thing happens with our audiences. If I say that I have three key messages for you today, how many can you focus on at once? The reality is that while most of us like to believe that we're excellent multitaskers, we're not. We have a finite amount of attention, and when we're doing more than one thing, we're spreading that attention across multiple tasks. The more places to focus our attention, the thinner it gets. When I speak, I want all of my audience's attention on one message—my point, my central idea. I do the hard job of figuring out where to place the audience's attention for them.

There are a few reasons why people have multiple messages, but the two most common reasons are because (1) they don't know what their point is, and (2) they aren't confident enough to have the spotlight on one central idea; the ownership is too great, the risk too high, their courage too low.

Own your idea. Feel confident about what you are saying, and let others know that you are willing to own it. Yes, this means if you're wrong, you own that, but it also means that when you're right, you get to own that, too. Remember that sharing an idea is a demonstration of leadership; the outcome, whether your idea flies or not, is less important.

THANK YOU

Hey there, you're a great reader! You might be thinking a variety of responses, I'll guess a few. "Not really, this is the first book I've read all year." "No, I'm not, I can only read a chapter a day!" "I'm not a good reader, my friend Alycia is." Hey, reader, try this one out ... thank you! Most compliments people give you are genuine and deserve to be received with thanks. Compliments are a gift that someone is trying to give you. When you discredit a compliment, in essence, you are rejecting it. Consider the parallel to any other type of gift. Imagine that I bring you a small box, and I hand it to you. Rejecting a compliment would be the same as slapping the box out of my hand. I'm sure we'd all agree that would be rude. Learn to say thank you and stop there. Not "Thank you, but—" Simply, thank you.

LEADER

Leader sounds like a big title, one that requires authority, but that's only one way to be a leader. Some think that to be a leader, you need to have direct reports—be the boss of one or more people. But there's another way you can be assigned the title of leader.

Consider this: A leader is a person who can inspire new thinking and behaviour in others. It's having an idea, sharing it with someone, and seeing them do something because of your idea. Here's an example: "The way I see it, now is the time to hire another intern. Here's why I say that: Students are beginning their final semester and are looking at intern postings. Moving on this now ensures we get the best pick. That's why I'm saying now is the time. Let's draft up the role description together and get it off to the university." Their response: "OK, makes sense." Their behaviour, meeting with you to prepare the posting.

There you have it—leadership in action. Have you ever done anything like that? I bet you have. So go ahead, call yourself a leader.

This language ties into a few other chapters of this book, namely chapter seven, "Kraft Dinner," and the final chapter. Chapter seven because, as I mentioned, communicating with strong language can be uncomfortable at first, and that chapter is focused on getting comfortable being uncomfortable. It'll reinforce what I'm saying here, which is: *do it*, in baby steps at first, but do it.

Intentionally use these words, and watch how they benefit you. The results will give you the encouragement you need to use them even more.

The final chapter is all about self-promotion, and speaking in confident language is key to doing that. If you want me to believe you're capable, smart, and determined, your language had better tell me that.

Use good words in all areas of your life. Words matter.

CHAPTER 5

After Hours

I'm blonde and cute and playing in the big boy circles. So, I hear it all.

It's more implicit now; it's no longer overt ass-grabbing, it's much worse than that.

Writing a chapter that aims to help you to navigate corporate politics, slimy execs, and gender norms is not easy.

Ahhhh, deep breath. Not easy because it shouldn't be this way, we shouldn't have to conform, we shouldn't have to play power games, and we shouldn't have to play games according to their rules. But … we do. It's just "is what it is." And the only way that this will change is when the balance of power is, well, more balanced. We have to get there. We have a long way to go, and getting there requires us to be leaders in what remains a man's world.

There are so many leadership qualities that we as women come by quite naturally—good listeners; empathic; collaborators; planners; visionaries. And although women are hardwired to be connectors, we tend to undervalue the importance of professional relationships. Even though we might understand that they are important, we often self-exclude (or are excluded) from opportunities to strategically build relationships. There are many reasons for this; some are our own doing, but others are conditions established by social norms. Which means some will feel acceptable to you and others will not. Regardless of the reasons why we are sitting back from the relationship game, I'm going to work very hard to convince you that you must stop immediately and begin to treat relationship-building as a high priority, an unwritten part of your job description, a critical activity you must perform every day, and a challenge with which your brilliant strategic mind must engage.

Here's the bottom line: It doesn't matter where you work, what you do, or what level you're at in the organization; there will always be power dynamics at play. That's why connecting with others and building relationships is so critical. I used a word there that might have made you uncomfortable—*power*. Somewhere along the way, power got a bad rap. We don't want to be seen as power-hungry or power-trippers, or, for some of us, even power*ful*. Owning our full power can be intimidating, uncomfortable, unknown, and scary. I do believe that many of us shy away from our full power for these reasons; I know I do. Yeah, I do. I feel it often, the suppression of my full power. For me, it's a place where the imposter syndrome appears—am I ready for what might unfold when I unleash my full self? Are others ready? And here it is: what if I can't handle me? It's like taking on a big project and then wondering, "Do I have what it takes?" This is some twisted psychology, though, when the "do I have what it takes" is questioning my readiness to be myself. Seriously? Do I have what it takes to be the full, most powerful version of myself? Of course I do! Our mental models and socialization have firmly planted some deep-seeded roots of self-doubt, to the point that we question our ability to manage ourselves at maximum strength. This is why so many of us show up as weaker, lesser versions of ourselves. So here I am, writing this book, embracing the inevitable success it will bring me. Am I ready for it? Can I handle it? *I'd* better believe it.

I want you to think of power differently; think of it as influence that can sway others or tool us to motivate and inspire others. Power can make us think of wealth, influence, and authority, but it can also remind us of change-makers and thought leaders. Rather than avoid power or pretend it doesn't exist in relationships, you'll be better served by being able to recognize where the balance of power sits. Also, let it *empower* you to know that momentum does shift, power dynamics do shift, even within a relationship. It's sort of like a dance; one person is always leading, and you can alternate who is leading. The main point is to recognize that someone is always leading. Because power can shift, think of it as mutable: it can grow and shrink; it can be shared, passed, held, gained, or given away. I believe that by empowering others, we increase our power. That's to say, by sharing my power with others, my power grows. Some would say the number one job of a leader is to develop other leaders, and I subscribe to that thinking. Leaders used to aspire to be branded with words such as strong, determined, and decisive, but those were the days when top-down, authoritative leadership was in vogue. Today, servant leadership is considered to be the most effective mindset to adopt when seeking to lead an organization. It is predicated on the thinking that leaders exist only to serve those whom they lead. The best leaders today are described as humble, vulnerable, curious, and courageous.

Because power exists within relationships, politics are at play. Uh-oh, I just used another hated word: *politics*. This word makes us think of politicians, games, dishonesty, secrets, winners, and losers. And phrases like *corporate politics, being politically savvy,* and *navigating political landscapes* (or land mines). None of this is appealing to most of us. But here's the thing: opting out is not an option. You often hear people, particularly women, say things like, "Oh, I want no part of that. I'm not interested in politics within my organization. I just go to work, put my head down, and do a great job, and then I go home." Hopefully the first part of this chapter helped you realize that you are operating in an environment where power and politics exist. It's very important that, if nothing else, you become aware that you *are* in the game. If you believe you're opting out, you're not; you're just a passive player who is likely playing the game poorly.

Your current strategy might be to work hard, produce excellent results, and keep your focus on the "work," and hey, that's good! It'll help you to keep your job, although I do know a number of people who were hard workers and great producers who got fired. Why? Poor team dynamics, ineffective working relationships, or sometimes even something as simple as not *likeable*. Look, results matter, but they are only part of the formula and, dare I say, not the most heavily weighted. You don't get promoted because you do good work; you get paid because you do good work. You get promoted because of the relationships you hold.

At this point, you might be thinking one of the following rebuttals:

1. I have no interest in amassing more power.
2. I am not seeking a promotion.
3. I work in a role that doesn't interact with others, so none of this matters to me.
4. Leaders in my company are not good at this, so why should I have to be?
5. I've seen people advance in my company who were not political.

I'll address each of these below.

1. I have no interest in amassing more power.

Why is that? Do you view power as a negative thing? Consider this: how might power help you achieve your goals, do your job better, and possibly even make a difference? We've seen Ruth Bader Ginsburg and Malala Yousafzai find their voices and use their power for good. If you don't know who either of these women are, put this book down and google them immediately. Power doesn't have to be self-serving; in fact, it has a multiplier on it when it's shared for the greater good.

2. I am not seeking a promotion.

You say you don't want a promotion? No problem! I will open a can of worms here, though. *Why* don't you want a promotion? Is it because you don't want to work more hours? Are you afraid of taking on the additional responsibility? Are you anxious about the work/life pressure that a more senior role may create? You've probably seen some leaders above you who work long hours, travel a lot, and seem to bear the weight of responsibility—heavy is the head that wears the crown. And although I personally have only ever pursued advancement, I can empathize with the very real leeriness many women have towards chasing or accepting senior leadership roles.

I coached a woman in the energy sector who was being groomed for a promotion. Her company specifically hired me to get her ready for her inevitable promotion. So, you can imagine my surprise when I learned she was tapped for the director role and turned it down. Her reason? She wasn't prepared to take on more while balancing her family life. She said she believed she'd be ready for it in a few years. Here's the unfortunate part: she wasn't going to be (re)-offered that role in a few years ... or ever. She passed it up, and they would now pass her up. Her reality was now that if she wanted a senior role, she'd very likely have to go elsewhere. Do I think she made the wrong decision? It doesn't matter what I think; what matters is that this story outlines a few points I hope you've picked up on.

First, there seems to be a widely accepted assumption that the more senior you are in the company, the harder you have to work. This is not always the case. The work is different, and the responsibility and accountability do increase. Your team may grow, and your title will change, but that does not necessarily equal more hours or effort than what you're putting into your current role. That's a secret people who are higher up don't want you to know.

Second, no one is ever ready for what comes next, even our male counterparts. There will always be parts of the job that you have to learn: adjustments to family and work schedules, new teams and projects to lead. The leap will never feel as smooth as you'd like, and you'll never be as prepared as you would like. Don't wait for the right time: it will never be the right time.

Still don't want a promotion? Fine. I'm going to ask you to reframe relationships as a means of achieving your highest potential within the role you have.

3. I work in a role that doesn't interact with others.

I have to challenge this one. Unless you are self-employed and only selling widgets to people via technology with absolutely no customer service, you do have a role that interacts with others and, at least to some degree, relies on relationships for success. Even if your work is to volunteer at a food bank, power and politics are at play. You see, it's not what you do, the role you have, or the company you work for—it's social constructs that make it so.

4. Leaders in my company are not good at this, so why should I have to be?
Yes, they are.

5. I've seen people advance in my company who were not political.
Keep watching. They were, and they will be.

Your skills and experience are important. Business results matter, but allow me to further dispel this concept of meritocracy, which points to a person's capabilities and merits as a means of garnering power and promotion. To do so, let's look at how advancement is typically determined. You've heard about the list, right? The list ... the one in the top drawer of your boss' desk, the one with a few names on it, the names of the people he or she is eyeing for advancement. The list might be titled "emerging leaders" or "hi-po's" (which means high-potential people). Basically, if you want to advance, you've got to be on this list, I promise. So, how do you get on that list? To find the answer, let's consider what leaders think about when selecting people to be on their leadership team. Spoiler alert: It's not how good you are at your job. Sorry.

Let's take this to a primal level. Evolutionary psychology tells us that whether it was sorting food or people, categorizing makes life simpler. It's like when you go grocery shopping. You don't review every option before making a selection; doing so would be time wasted, when you've already made a decision about what you like. Instead, categorizing likes helps you make the choice instantly. For example, you're walking down the grocery aisle and you need spaghetti sauce. Do you read the back of every label? Or do you have one or two favourites? Having your preferences helps make you more efficient.

It's why we have a circle of friends and a network. We don't wake up every day and face the daunting task of recasting our circle every day; instead, categorizing likes helps you make the choice instantly. In hunter-gatherer days, the quicker you made decisions like these, the more likely you were to survive. And this remains true today.

From there, we developed sorting criteria which helps us to make decisions quickly, by evaluating others' appearances, communication, and behaviour. We subconsciously determine who's in and who's out. "Research has shown that managers sort their employees into winners and losers as early as three weeks after starting to work with them."*

We are also hardwired to think of ourselves first and to like ourselves best. Because we are most familiar with ourselves, we are most comfortable with others that most closely reflect ourselves back to us. The further the deviation away from ourselves, the less comfortable we are, and if being in your presence makes me uncomfortable, I'm probably not promoting you to my executive team. That's how you get executive teams that all look the same and have all the same background, because what we've done is surround ourselves with the people who make us feel the most comfortable. With most people in power being men, women are biologically up against some challenges. This explains why only now we're beginning to see faces other than male, white, 60ish-year-old ones (sometimes called pale, male, and stale) around the corporate executive and board tables. There are unconscious biases. Some are due to what I've described, a quest for likeness, and others are due to biases around what a leader can and should look like. There are still people who believe that if a person comes to work with a nose ring, that they are not going

---

* Nigel Nicholson, "How Hardwired is Human Behavior?" *Harvard Business Review*, July–August 1998, https://hbr.org/1998/07/how-hardwired-is-human-behavior.

to be a hard worker, that there will never be a spot for them on the leadership team, and they are not to be taken seriously. Those are judgements and perceptions, biases in this person's brain that are telling them they do not fit the mold as a leader ... simply because they have a ring in their nose. Before President Obama, if I said close your eyes and describe what you see when you imagine the President of the United States, most of you would describe a white man. What about a doctor? A teacher? An executive? These biases, or mental shortcuts, play a role in informing not only others' views of our pro-motability but the roles in which we cast ourselves. Many books have been written on unconscious biases; this is not one of them. If you wish to learn more about unconscious bias, I encourage you to do so.

Creating an organization that is diverse and inclusive requires leaders to embrace discomfort for the greater good and to assign real value to diverse thought, diverse perspective, and diverse leadership. With that needs to come the establishment of inclusionary social norms; the development of new norms that are more universally respectful. Leaders need to be aware of the fact that these biases exist in our brains, be convinced that there is value in difference, and put mechanisms in place that balance or offset these tendencies.

Story time. I was on a short flight one night and found myself sitting next to an older woman who looked, well, unkempt. She was filthy—her clothes were dirty, her hair was a mess, and her fingernails were packed with dirt. I'll admit, I thought I was sitting next to a homeless woman. I was tired, and although I've worked supporting homeless people for many years, I didn't feel like engaging. I wasn't put off by her; I just really didn't feel up for the chat. So, *lots* of assumptions made here, and they were all based on my unconscious biases. Her appearance informed my perception of who she was as a person and what engaging with her might mean for the rest of my flight. Well, despite my best efforts to avoid eye contact and connection with her, she got me talking, and am I ever glad she did. Guess what?!?! She was NOT a homeless person. She was flying home from a multi-month project she was working on in China as a coal miner. *A coal miner.* Hence the dirt. As my eyes opened and my heart softened, my preconceived notions dropped, and my ears were ready to listen and learn. In that moment, I became an inclusive leader—one who was humbled and curious. Having done a good amount of consulting in the mining industry developing women leaders, I began peppering her with questions about her experience as a coal miner in China. We talked for an hour, and I didn't want our conversation to end, but she left me with a profound comment. She said that she hopes to live to see the day when her work and her role as a woman miner are no longer seen as "remarkable." She didn't want women in mining to be unusual, striking, or extraordinary. She applauded the work I'm doing to help develop women in male-dominated industries. We committed to each of us doing our part on that quest, and when we parted ways, I cried. It was powerful.

So, where does this leave us? Don't worry, I'm not going to suggest that you wear the corporate uniform of a grey suit and white shirt. Heck no, embrace your own style! I am going to talk about the other aspects of relationship-building, which we can achieve without looking or acting like men.

You may have heard terms like "political savviness" or "navigating the corporate landscape." These are a fancy way of talking about playing "the game." I've talked about the game, but now I'm going to break down the rules, or you may unknowingly break those rules or miss a chance to win, and frankly, I see women lose at this game far too often.

The measurement of how you're doing in the game is called *polit-*

ical capital, and I want you to think about it as a bank account. Like an account, political capital has credits and debits. You can spend it and earn it. The person with the most political capital at any given point is winning, so clearly, we need to focus on earning, and be cautious about our spending. How do you get credits? Many ways! You can earn through delivering great results on a project (and making sure people know about it), winning new business (and making sure people know about it), creating a new product or service line and (making sure people know about it), demonstrating your talent in front of senior people, or leading a winning team (and making sure people know about it). Ummmm, notice a trend? Self-promotion. So many times, women have wins and keep them to themselves, like secret prizes, and it is not serving us well—we're losing the game.

Now, let's look at how debits occur in your political capital. You might assume it's through making mistakes, losing business, or otherwise screwing up. Wrong! Here's what men seem to get that we women don't: political capital is not exclusively, or even predominately, tied to performance. It's anchored in the strength of relationships with people who hold the power—let's call them the *judges* of the game; after all, they ultimately determine who is winning. So, the trick to winning the game is to manage the judges' perception of you at all times.

There's another way we can earn credits and win the game, and that is through leveraging others' political capital. I know, who would give us their credits? They're called *sponsors*, and they don't give it away; they see it as an investment that will earn them even more capital. They expect a return. You might be wondering, "Who are these angels, and where do I find one?" Well, think of them as angel investors, strategic power shifters, and they are right in front of you … at work.

Sponsors are people in your organization, or at the very least, in your industry, who have amassed power and have a nice-looking bank account of political capital. They've been where you are and have had their own sponsors to get where they are. They know they can earn even more capital by finding gems to spotlight and gleaning some of their shine. Because of this, they are always on the hunt for gems. How do you get a sponsor? Be a gem.

How to be a gem = work equally as hard at developing relationships with potential sponsors as you do driving great results at work. When they feel you're a safe bet, they'll invest. What happens next is that they will be your champion and greatest spokesperson. They will speak well of you at senior tables, offer your name as an emerging leader, get you a promotion, and when it happens, they're counting on you to knock it out of the park—that's when they get their return. Imagine how this plays out long-term. You've climbed the ladder, thanks, in part, to their sponsorship, and they are at or near the helm. They now have alliances that they can use to increase the reach of their power across the organization through you. Power-massing. Smart. Strategic. Again, if you're reading this and thinking, "Shit, this sounds like a lot of effort that would be better spent on just doing great work," consider this: leaders rely on power to steer the ship and to influence and inspire others to follow their vision. Call it a necessary evil if you want, but the bottom line is, without powerful, strategic leadership, organizations would be no more than a bunch of people doing really good work … all rowing, not in unison, and without direction.

There comes a time when the ability to win at this game becomes paramount, and that is when you're in a leadership role. As I said, power is an important lever for a leader, yet many people become leaders through strong performance as a contributor or as a subject matter expert. I see it all of the time. Engineers who get promoted over and over and ultimately become COO's, and then frantically search out an executive coach to teach them how to do their new job—which is to lead. You see, as senior leaders, what got them there is no longer needed; COO's don't do engineering—they lead. Along with navigating the political environment, they now must learn how to create a vision, set strategy, communicate in an inspiring way, engage their workforce, and other crucial leadership skills, none of which they learned in engineering school. My advice to you is to begin getting good at these skills now, regardless of your current role or profession, and as you develop your leadership, a funny thing might happen.... You could be seen as a gem.

Sponsors are not the same as *mentors*. I began by talking about sponsorship for a reason, and that is because research shows that women are over-mentored and under-sponsored, and it's giving our male counterparts a huge advantage. Mentors are important, too. I have a few who have helped to shape my life, provided me with incredible wisdom, and genuinely cared for me, and I am exceptionally grateful for them. They are Cynthia Pearson and Mike McCarron. Mentors provide guidance, share stories, listen, and may offer suggestions. Sponsors get you promoted. See the difference? Both relationships are needed and are key to your success. Make it your business to secure both.

Since relationships are key to our success, obviously I'm going to tell you to network. Yeah, sort of. Networking usually means inserting yourself into industry events, attending conferences, and basically tossing business cards around. If doing that seems senseless and a waste of time, well, you're right, it is when it's not done right. I figured out how to network strategically (the hard way), and I want to give you back hundreds of hours by telling you what I learned.

When I first began consulting in the field of women's leadership development, I was living in Vancouver and shot out of the gate fast! I enthusiastically signed myself up for every, and I mean *every*, networking opportunity I could find. How fun, I thought.

Here are my observations that led me to decide these events were a waste of my time (and yours).

1. Most of the people there already knew each other.
2. There was wine and, sometimes, cheese.
3. These events were usually held after work hours.
4. They were poorly funded and attended (see #3).
5. There were no men; it was all women.

So, other than the free wine and, sometimes, cheese, I almost always left with nothing. No new meaningful connections, no new learning. Sure, the socially brave could lubricate themselves with the wine and infiltrate the already established cliques, but what about the others? The lack of intention, planning, budget, and male support was, frankly, offensive, and it infuriated me. Still does. Remember this: standing around and drinking wine with people you already know is not networking; it's drinking wine with friends, and it does not require corporate branding, but thanks anyway. The only thing worse than doing nothing is pretending to do something.

What about conferences? They seem well-organized, with good speaker lineups and name tags; this should be better, right? Maybe. I've been working with women for over 15 years, and still today, one of the biggest challenges is establishing work/life balance (or whatever it's called these days). This is why I am asking you to be discerning about where and how you spend your time. Time is more valuable than money, yet we so carelessly throw it away without monitoring the spend. You can make more money; you can't make more time, yet we spend a lot of time managing money. I'm going to help squeeze some time out of your spend and give it back to you. This book has a time-back guarantee.

Here's the secret to spending time wisely: Be entirely selfish. Review every invitation and ask yourself, "What will I get out of this?" In assessing invitations, I want you to consider two things: who will be there and what might you learn. When I say who will be there, I don't mean who will be there that you can snuggle up to for the night, but who will be there that presents an opportunity for you. See? Be selfish. This might be someone you've never met but would like to meet. It could be someone you have an established relationship with but would like to build upon it. Or it could be to intentionally spend time maintaining a solid relationship with someone who is key to your success—like an important client, a mentor, or an industry leader. If you're not going to the event with any of these intentions, then don't go. Tip: You can email the event organizers in advance and request a list of delegates, and they will almost always give it to you. You're welcome.

Next, consider what you might learn. Events with strong agendas will have some thought leadership to share, speakers who know their stuff (like me), and takeaways you can apply to your world right away. Commit to making full use of this time by intentionally seeking out new learning. Review the agenda and speaker list, and set some learning objectives for yourself.

Bottom line, you have to take control of how you spend your time, and squeeze value out of every opportunity. With this rule as my guide, I am much more strategic about accepting invitations to networking events, and when I'm there, I am laser focused on deriving value.

Once you've selfishly determined an event will present opportunity for you, you need to prepare to work it, and preparing begins before you get there. Let me walk you through my process. I was attending a mining conference in Toronto, and while I'd done a fair bit of consulting in the industry, this was a group that presented a good opportunity for me. While some would walk into that conference and aim to throw 500 business cards in the air, I was much more strategic. My preparation began by finding out who would be there and identifying who I wanted to connect and build a connection with. Once I knew who I was after, I thought about how I could get to them—where would they be? Who do I know who could provide a warm introduction to them? How could I get in front of them and ultimately get them alone for a brief meeting? If possible, I found answers to all of these questions before the event.

Considering my targets, I selected my attire and considered everything from contacts or glasses, suit or business dress, hair down or up—all of this was going to contribute to their perception of me and my brand, and we all know the importance of first impressions. On that note, a senior woman leader once told me a good rule: if you can see up it, down it, or through it, it's not appropriate for business. So, I tossed aside my sheer blouse and miniskirt and opted for a navy suit with a white shirt. I was going to be approaching senior executives, and they'd be in suits; I'd be, too. I needed them to see me as one of them, not an assistant or a booth babe. This was not the time to be sexy or cute; it was the time to be polished and confident.

Alright, so now I'm dressed.

I'm there; what next? I'll tell you this: showing up is not enough. Waiting for people to approach you isn't enough. Passively participating isn't enough. Now is the time to call upon your courage and determination and push yourself out of your comfort zone. People like to be prepared (women even more so than men); it minimizes risk and makes us feel more comfortable in these high-stakes situations. So go ahead, prepare! Since these people are important to me, it makes sense that I'd give some thought about what I'm going to say when I actually get in front of them. Do some homework. Visit their LinkedIn, their company website, google their company and select "news"—read up. Call people who know them and find out what you can. Sounds like stalking, OK, it's not far off, but with really honest intentions. Find out about their current business projects, charitable passions, and career history, and look for common ground you can use as small talk to kick off your conversation. Tip: Asking people about themselves is always a good idea; it's our favourite topic. Ego and all....

Prepare to have a few probing questions for them to keep the conversation going; be prepared to be a listener; get them talking. And, above all else, have your ask prepared. What is it you want from them when the conversation comes to an end? In most cases, networking events are not the time to engage in heavy business talk or seek to close deals. Instead, use this time to secure the meeting where that will happen. For me at the mining conference, my ask was just that: to have their agreement to meet with me following the event.

I didn't go home from that event with 500 new business cards that represented surface-level interactions. I went home with six new connections that represented real business opportunities. Yay me!

CHAPTER 6

Sticky Situations

Regardless of your personal circumstances, we know that women still tend to carry most of the home life responsibilities—grocery shopping, child rearing, house cleaning—and we do so in a way that puts ourselves last. This is concerning on many levels, and since we already covered self-care in another chapter, I'm going to discuss how this impacts our ability to succeed in the corporate politics game. Here, we're going to apply what we now know about power and politics and the need for relationship-building to common yet challenging situations.

Some (most) industries are referred to as being male-dominated, but we are all living and working in a male-dominated culture. Society uses male-dominated language (*firemen*, *congressmen*), and in almost every way that counts it positions men as superior. With this, most relationship-building opportunities are designed to accommodate men and inconvenience women. Six p.m. cocktails? Cool, who feeds the kids? Hubby is out playing pool with the guys from work. Seven a.m. squash game? Cool, who takes the kids to school, hubby is golfing with members of his club. Oh, what's that? You don't have a husband or children? Me neither, so I guess we can make it to all of those invites. But what if you have a dog to walk, a yoga class to attend, or heck, you just want to sleep in and you can't stand racquet sports? What if the invite to have drinks was at a strip club? What if you don't drink? What if you are other gendered or have other sexual orientations? Yeah, so because of all of that, we need to develop positive, self-respecting ways to build the relationships that are necessary to advance or to work to your fullest potential.

I almost wrote a whole book on this, and it was going to be called *The Dark Side of Business Travel*. I began travelling for work in my early thirties, and honestly, I had no idea what the world was like. I'd done some travelling before, had lived in different parts of the country, and would've considered myself to be somewhat street smart, but in this realm, I was like the most naïve little girl in the entire world. Frankly, I was unprepared to discover what I learned about the big adult world of corporate business. If you think business travelling is all about fancy dinners and cute, smelly hotel soaps, you'd better keep reading. There are land mines all around that I want you to be aware of for your safety and so that you can develop strategies to play the politics game with your integrity intact. You'll be faced with excessive drinking, drugs, infidelity, abused expense accounts, and *a lot* of partying. Sound like a frat party? Pretty much, except the booze is top shelf.

No one likes a free meal and a glass or two of red wine after a flight more than me, but the rest of these "relationship-building" tactics aren't my scene. I'm going to share some real-life examples of gender-bias situations and offer some strategies for dealing with them.

"Unwine" Time

I often travel on my own for business, and when I am dining alone, one of my strategies is to find the hotel bar/restaurant/lounge and create a safe environment for myself. You see, I'd learned that hotel restaurants are full of others (mostly men) who are also dining alone but don't want to be. I've been approached quite aggressively by many men, who've asked to join me for a drink and propositioned much more. I found these situations uncomfortable and became tired of having to enforce my boundaries every time I wanted a bite of my salmon, so I developed a new strategy—I recruited help. I sat at the bar and became very chummy with the bartenders. Once they were on my side, I'd ask them to look out for me by telling them what my boundaries were. I would tell them that I don't accept drinks from anyone, and if a guy said he wanted to send me a drink, they'd tell him the answer is no—she's buying her own drinks tonight. If I had to leave to go to the bathroom, they would take my drink and put it behind the bar. They watched out for me. When I was leaving, they'd make sure I was OK; they were like a big brother. I developed that. I developed those relationships for my own safety.

Throw One Back

In Carly Fiorina's book, *Tough Choices: A Memoir* (Fiorina, 2006), she describes many coping mechanisms and strategies she had to employ to keep herself safe while travelling or doing business in different cultures. Fiorina talks about her business experiences in Asia, including entertaining and drinking with clients. "Over the years, I would participate in many drinking rituals in Korea, Japan, and China. I would learn to prepare myself mentally, to prepare myself physically by eating the right kinds of foods ahead of time and to toss liquor straight back in my throat, not sip it, so that the alcohol is absorbed more slowly into the system." Quick tip, drinking water helps, too. You can either have a glass of water at your table or swing by the bar on the way to the washroom and grab a glass. She knew these rituals and shared experiences were an important aspect of building trusting relationships and would make it easier to do business with her Chinese business associates in the future, but she also knew that only she could ensure her safety. Finding a balance, Fiorina managed her intake of alcohol as well as the need to show up as "tough enough" to be in the circle.

To party, or not to party...

An associate once told me that she and her senior manager were travelling for work together when he told her that he wanted to see her succeed. That night, he told her she needed to party with the client. The plan was that they were all going out for drinks, and then to someone's house. She told him she was tired and had work to do, but honestly, she confided to me that she was really uncomfortable with partying at a house with a bunch of men. "It just didn't feel safe," she said. He responded, "You have to party to impress the client." She was listening to her intuition and trying to enforce her boundaries, but found it very challenging to know what to do. Ultimately, she stayed in her hotel room and worked, but we don't know what, if any, damage that may have caused to the perception her boss and client had of her for doing so. I know, it shouldn't matter, but it does.

Skip Dessert

My sister and I were at a restaurant one day and witnessed a group of three sit down—a boss (a guy), a man, and a woman—and the three of them had lunch. Then, as soon as the act of eating lunch was over, the woman, almost frantically, once the table was cleared, said something to the effect of, "I have a very big list of things to do, and have to get back to my desk and chew through that list." So, she left. As soon as she left (not because she left but after she left), the two men ordered a scotch and loosened their neckties, and the *actual* intention of having lunch began. Relationship-building took place. My guess? A year later, the male colleague got promoted, and the woman complained to friends that she, once again, got passed over for a greatly deserved promotion. She still believes getting her list of things done is more important than relationships, and until that changes, she will likely continue to get passed over for promotions. This is how it goes.

How Do I Look?

A female client of mine was in a helicopter with a top government leader. He didn't say a word to her for the duration of the flight. When they arrived, he was briefed by his communications people, and then they left the room, leaving her alone with him. He said, "What's your name? Is my tie straight? If I get on the news tonight and it's not straight, I'm going to find you. You have to touch it and make sure." Being ordered to touch someone is sexual harassment, and you don't ever have to do it. My client knew how inappropriate this was, said "You look fine," and left the room.

Tee vs. "Tea" Time

A woman I coached works in insurance, and for much of her career, she's been with big, global insurance companies. She told me of a team-building/social day her company had planned, and because I love that shit, I couldn't wait to hear all about it. She was much less thrilled. The company had two activities planned: golf (for the guys) and tea (for the ladies). This story is made funnier by knowing my client, who is not the tea party type at all. It made me think about the loaded assumptions that went into the planning of this team-building day. Let's list them!

- All men like golf.
- All women like tea.
- There is no value in team-building between genders.

OK, back to my client, who doesn't drink tea and would rather golf, not because she enjoys golf but because she knows the value in out-of-office time with senior leaders, who were mostly men and who would all be on the golf course. Not much of a surprise ending here; my client golfed, but to get there, she had to find the courage to challenge the biases, norms, and status quo. Not all of us have this courage, which is why these events continue to be planned as such.

Lack of inclusion often perpetuates exclusive behaviours and gender biases. Advocate for yourself; no one else will.

A Swing Around a Pole

Ever been invited to a strip club as a company event? I have. I was at a client's conference in Florida, and after the official evening activities, a group was continuing the party and invited me along. I didn't know I was heading to a strip club until we arrived. Once out of the cab, I had a decision to make, go in, or go back to the hotel. So much played into this decision—relationships, values, personal comfort, safety. What I hadn't considered was how others might be feeling, probably due to my focus on my own self-preservation. Through this experience, I've come to realize that many men are also uncomfortable in that environment. Some, because they value women too much to view them merely as objects there for their entertainment. Others, because they are fathers or brothers, who find it hard not to associate the entertainment as someone else's daughter or sister. Others, because they are non-heterosexual, have religious beliefs or personal values that are repulsed by the whole industry, and feel strongly that it is a heinous, disrespectful thing to participate in. So, back to that night: seven of us had just piled out of two taxis. Those, like me, who were not in the know, took a moment to get their bearings, and shortly after, one guy quickly suggested another pub across the street, touting their amazing wings and draft deals. Without another thought, we all pivoted and walked across the street. Look, whether you personally enjoy strip clubs or not is not the issue here; it's that they are absolutely not an appropriate business off-site, relationship-building location. Let's all agree that if an event, situation, or location segregates others or makes people uncomfortable in any way, it is not good for business.

Mother, May I?

We all face challenging situations. Pregnant women and mothers have it even tougher. Here are a few scenarios that will give you an idea of what I'm talking about.

Elephant in the Room

As part of a consulting project, we interviewed employees and leaders to deepen our understanding of their current level of inclusivity practices. One of the interviews was with the company's COO. After a brief chat, he said, "Let's just address the elephant in the room. Women can have babies, and men can't." I said, "True." He said, "That puts women at a huge disadvantage. When I'm looking to invest in developing a successor or an emerging leader, I can't risk that person leaving for a mat leave."

Empty Frames

A client told me she never puts pictures of her children on her desk. Why? Because there is a socially constructed perceived reality that she couldn't do both—be a leader and a mother at the same time.

Hands Off

One of my associates told me about a situation that happened when she was working for a consulting company and was pregnant. At her boss's retirement party, he came up to her, felt her belly (without asking), and said, "It's too bad that you are pregnant, because you would have been promoted."

This shit happens. Every day. Your gender is not an excuse to hold us back. It's time we find a way to build relationships, stand up for ourselves, and start to be seen as the leaders we are.

Many diversity groups are overlooked when companies plan well-intended social events or other relationship-building opportunities. These bias-ridden situations are not reserved exclusively for women. Here are a few disastrous examples.

Lucky Winner

I co-wrote and facilitated a course called "Proud to Lead," aimed at equipping and empowering the LGBTQ community to be heard and seen as leaders. In this pilot of this program, a gay man shared a story that rocked me and changed him. He worked for a global accounting firm, and at their annual holiday party, he was the lucky winner of the big prize—a trip to Hawaii! He excitedly took the stage, and in front of the entire company, the leader handing out the prize said this into the microphone, "Paul, you must be ecstatic! You can now take your wife on a fabulous trip!"

All of the joy was sucked out of Paul at that very moment. He had a decision to make: say, "Indeed!" and walk off the stage, *or* correct the inaccuracy. The latter would mean coming out to his boss and the entire company, but he believed that not doing so would be denying himself. There isn't a right way to handle these situations; it's personal, but this is my very point: it's personal. An innocent mistake on the leader's part, perhaps, but one that we all need to be much more aware of, so they happen less often. Paul chose to come out to 1,600 people on that stage that night. I'm not sure I would've had his courage.

Share a Meal

Nothing brings a team together quite like eating together. That's why holiday potlucks at lunch are a thing. We've evolved as a society and are beginning to draw greater awareness about allergies and other dietary restrictions, but how about other considerations? At one of my client's offices, they chose to host a company potluck during Ramadan, a holy month of fasting, introspection, and prayer for Muslims. And, yes, there was a Muslim man on the team. Good intentions, but not inclusive.

Opting Out Does Not Mean Opting Out

Such situations leave one begging the question, "How can I still be who I am as a woman, as a mother, as a partner, but still invest the time and energy into developing relationships that are necessary for me to be successful in life?" It often feels like there has to be a trade-off, and either way, we lose. Either we have to sacrifice our values (and possibly our safety), or we have to miss out and miss the chance to get ahead. Well, I have very good news for you. Opting out of activities that are not a fit for you does not mean you have to opt out of building strategic relationships.

The fact is that men designed the corporate world we live in today. They are at the top, and they established the corporate culture and professional social norms. These norms favour men. Fortunately, some of this is changing, due to more women at the top (barely) and more men involved in family life (barely). So perhaps we'll begin to see more inclusivity out of office, but until then, I'm going to tell you how you can do it your way and succeed.

You can build relationships in self-respecting ways. It's not necessary to abandon who you are and behave in a way that is not aligned to your values. Even though in a lot of male-dominated industries it may feel that way from time to time, that said, we as women need to realize that if we're not going to take up golf and can't (or choose not to) go for drinks with the boss after work, we'd better find another way to develop those relationships. Remember: You can't opt out. I don't believe we should have to do things we are uncomfortable with or participate in unsafe situations or even activities we're just not interested in, but based on all you learned in the previous chapter, I'm sure you understand now that you *do* have to figure out a way.

> "There is always one true inner voice. Trust it."
> —Gloria Steinem, *Revolution From Within* (Steinem, 1993)

Let me introduce you to a model you can use to help you navigate these sticky situations. It's called the STAR model. STAR is an acronym, and it stands for *Stop, Think, Act,* and *Review*. This model will help you to make values-based decisions that will help you not only survive these situations but emerge and be seen as a leader.

It begins with *Stop*, asking us to pause. For most of us, this is the hardest part. We are faced with a challenge, something that is emotional or contentious, and our initial response is to react. But we know that often our impulsive reactions are just that—reactions—and not well-thought-through. Because of this, they might not be the ideal or best response we could give in the situation, leaving us with regret. Perhaps our reaction was fueled with an emotion that, while honourable, didn't serve us well. Here's an example: someone says something hurtful to you and your reaction is to hurt back out of your hurt. Instead, stopping, pausing, can give us the space we need to move from reacting from purely an emotional place and instead make use of our minds.

During this Stop phase, while you're pausing, I want you to use the time to do a few things that will radically change the outcome of the situation. First, assess safety. In some cases, you or others may not be safe to remain in the situation. So, pause and create space. Determine whether you need to take time (a minute, a day) to digest the situation and think through your response. You have the right to do that, always.

Once you're safe and ready to engage, I want your very next move to be to get curious, to ask questions, to listen, and to learn. Yes, even when someone is agitating you.

Listening is something we all think we're really great at, but we're not. It takes more than ears and the ability to hear to listen. It takes attention and intention. Active listening is called that because it's something that requires action and participation. Listening, fully present and without distractions. Listening to understand, not to respond. Most people listen for the first bit of someone talking, and then we assume the rest. We assume we know where they are going with what they are saying, so instead, we employ what we've determined to be a more efficient use of everybody's time, and we use their bit and our assumption and begin to prepare our response. This is not active listening. It's barely even basic listening. Of course, the danger in this way of listening is that we get it wrong; our assumptions of what they were trying to tell us are wrong. Then we respond with what we've prepared, and it's not an appropriate response to what they said. The speaker would naturally feel frustrated and probably say something like, "Were you even listening to me?" As a leader, this risk of getting it wrong is something we can manage. If we truly want to understand others' positions, thoughts, attitudes, and feelings, we need to listen—the whole way through. When the speaker is finished is when we can do our thinking about our response, and not until then. This requires us to listen fully, pause (yes, this means a moment of silence will occur, and I promise the speaker will wait), and then respond. Do you have someone in your life who listens to you this way? If so, it's very likely that they are your favourite person in the world to talk to. Being heard, truly heard, is rare, and when we experience it, it feels as good as getting a hug.

Listening gives you an incredible advantage; it provides you with intel. To get to a place where you and the speaker can engage in a conversation, the "temperature" needs to drop. Since we can only control our own actions, the job of diffusing the situation falls to you.

There are three steps in this de-escalation process, and tip: these work with every kind of situation, personal and professional.

First, I want you to disarm the speaker by finding *something* that they are saying that you can agree with. Begin your disarm statement with a phrase like "You're right." Why? Well, it's impossible to argue with someone who is agreeing with you. Seek to find common ground, and you will be on your way to diffusing the situation. Let's run this de-escalation process through an example. Let's use the *Hands Off* situation, the one where the boss said too bad you're pregnant, 'cause you would have been promoted. Gut reaction? Perhaps some would verbally punch back with a comment like "Too bad you're being replaced by a younger, smarter person," but punching back only feels good in the moment and does not see us leaving a leadership impression. Some might have cried quietly later at home. But what if, instead, you responded with, "You're right. I am pregnant." No "but," stop there, and pause. What might that have done to the temperature of the interaction? It's unexpected, it's professional, it's non-confrontational, and above all else, it's common ground—something both of you can agree on. I know, I know, you're thinking: WHAT?!?!?! You want me to agree with this jerk? Yes, I do. For now. Stay with me.

Next, construct and deliver an empathetic statement. A statement that shows how you connect with the thinking or feeling behind what the other person is saying. Showing empathy here is the "two" of the one-two de-escalation punch, and it works like a charm. Here are a couple of options to show what an empathetic statement can be in our example: "You see my pregnancy as a disadvantage" or "I'm sure this takes me out of the running in your eyes." Notice that both of these are assumptions; they are safe and show clear alignment with the thinking behind what the speaker was saying. Also important to note is that you must resist the urge to say these empathetic statements in a condescending way. We're not aiming to "get him back," make him feel bad, or mock his position. We're aiming to show understanding of his thought processes, so be sure to deliver these statements in that vein, with compassion. At this point, I'm sure you're thinking, "Why the hell would I want to show compassion to someone who has clearly disrespected me, undervalued me, and insulted me?!" Well, again, stay with me.

The final step in the de-escalation process is to seek to further your understanding about the other person's thinking. Why? Because soon you're going to aim to inspire new thinking in them, and doing so requires a clear line of sight into their current position. To do this, you're going to ask probing questions as and when needed. These are questions necessary to clarify and deepen your understanding of their thinking. In our example, these questions might include:

1. What leadership traits do you believe are required for the role?
2. Have you worked with or for a woman who failed as a leader because she was pregnant?
3. When I wasn't pregnant, what did you see in me that made you think I'd be good for the promotion?

Again, resist the urge to ask these probing questions in an attacking or condescending tone.

So, now you've stopped, paused, assessed your safety, listened, disarmed, offered an empathetic statement, and asked probing questions. You feel confident that you truly understand the speaker's position and are ready to challenge his thinking. Before you do, there's one more step, and that is to check in with yourself. This is where *Think* from the STAR model begins.

Our personal values are an authentic representation of our true selves and the link between our hearts and our minds. They describe who we are, our purpose, what we expect of ourselves, and what we expect of others. They can help us understand why and how we react to certain situations, and they can help guide our decision-making. If you aren't familiar with your personal values, I encourage you to acquaint yourself. There are workshops and free online resources that can help you with this.

Personal values are an important factor in handling challenging situations because they not only help us determine the best response, but they can also be at the root of our initial reaction. I first considered the role that values play in these situations when I was coaching a mid-career woman who wanted help suppressing her emotions at work. I hear this a lot, the desire to control one's emotions. I suppose this comes from the gender bias that we are more emotional than men, that we are basically basket cases walking around on the brink of tears, and that showing emotion, especially crying, is a career-limiting move. This just in: feeling and showing emotion is normal, natural, and always OK.

I asked my client to tell me of a recent situation where she was emotional at work. She told me about a sales competition that happened the month before. The competition was issued by the sales leader, and my client was well positioned to finish at or near the top. Suddenly, the leader changed the rules. What it took to win had been changed at the final hour, and she was *not* happy. She stormed into her boss' office and exploded. She was full of rage, and then the tears came. She'd become overwhelmed with emotion. As she told me this story, she was full of regret, because, although changing the rules at the last minute was unfair, she wasn't proud of her reaction. She wanted to do better.

As she told me her story, it was clear to me that she felt deeply wronged. Her reaction was leaning toward the extreme. So, I began asking her probing questions (yes, to deepen my understanding of her feelings and thinking). What I learned was that fairness is one of her values. This explained her response. The closer a situation rubs up against one of your values, the more likely you are to have a strongly provoked response. Think of it like friction. As two elements rub, energy is generated, and kinetic energy is converted into thermal energy. Literally, things heat up.

The first step in dissipating the energy is to draw awareness to the source. This requires us to be aware that we have been provoked, are feeling an intense emotion, and remember that there is great value in being deliberate about our response. Therefore, the time you take to pause here will serve you well, I promise. In this case, if my client had paused and become aware that the change in rules was unfair and that fairness was one of her personal values, she might have been able to predict that her reaction would be strong and could have mitigated it. The second step is to weaken the energy by injecting countering logic and adapting her mindset. Yes, changing the rules of the game is unfair; however, she can choose to take some time, create some space, and look at the situation from a distance, weakening the friction. In this space, she could then consider points such as:

- This isn't a personal attack; it was an organizational decision.
- This is only a work contest, and my emotional wellbeing is more important.
- My power to change the situation lies in my response to it.
- I'll have the greatest influence by addressing the unfairness in a calm, leader-like manner.

Let's apply this values discussion to our *Hands Off* situation. Perhaps this pregnant woman felt her value of integrity was being challenged. If so, her impulse response might have been to swat his hands off her belly and scream at the guy. Using the STAR model, she'd have paused and considered her personal values. Realizing she's feeling an extreme emotion, she would have considered how her response can influence the outcome, and instead, decided to take a breath, pause, and think through her next move. There is power in pausing. I cannot stress this enough—there is power in the pause. There is power to be gained—for you and the other—in responding with a thoughtful, confident retort. Let's look at what else happens in the *Think* stage and what a leadership response might sound like in the *Hands Off* situation.

By now, you've taken time to determine if and how the situation might be rubbing up against your personal values. It's time to develop your message. Your message is one sentence. It's your point;

it's your headline. It's the main point you want to get across in your response, and to emphasize its importance and ensure it doesn't get lost in other parts of your response, you're going to open with it. Here's the tough part: it needs to be positive or, at the very least, not negative. Why? Because we want the receiver to focus on where we want them to go, how we want them to behave or think. Not to focus on what *not* to do. There are two ways to say everything, and positive positioning is much more effective.

A reminder of what her boss said to her.

"It's too bad that you are pregnant because you would have been promoted."

Here are a few messages that could be used in the *Hands-Off* situation:

1. I'm confident you will find that the skills you see in me, which make me well-suited for that promotion, are still present and strong.
2. You are right to see me as an emerging leader who's ready for advancement.
3. I'm sure you'll agree that my record and relationships are strong enough to bridge a maternity leave.
4. By focusing on my talent, you'll be as confident as I am that now is the time for my promotion.

A few things you might notice all of these messages have in common: They are confident, they are positive, and they are strong. They are not defensive, and they are not likely to be what would come out of your mouth on impulse. What makes them sound strong and confident is the language. Remember from the chapters on good words and bad words that *words matter*. Let's see how these messages would sound with weaker language, likely the kind of language you're using every day.

1. I'm pretty sure I have the skills needed for that promotion.
2. I suppose I am ready for advancement.
3. I think my record and relationships are strong enough to bridge a maternity leave.
4. I guess I'm ready for the promotion.

Much less confident, much less persuasive, and much less inspiring. When we're attempting to change someone's thinking or behaviour, we need to be more than contemplative. Inspiring others to have confidence in us, in our ideas, requires us to show confidence in ourselves.

Now you're ready to deliver your response and *Act,* entering the next stage of the STAR model. You've done great listening; you've empathized; you've probed to truly understand their position; and you've crafted a confident leadership message. Let's do this! It's time to deliver your message with conviction and strength. Once you've said it, pause. That's right, say your one sentence, and then stop talking. In your mind, you will feel ready to unleash all of the valid points that help you argue your message, but knowing where to start requires you to, once again, listen. After you say your message, the other person will do one of four things: agree (unlikely), be curious and say something like, "Tell me more," disagree, or say nothing. What you say next must be in response to their response. If they agree, ask them to do something that demonstrates they are aligned with your thinking. In our example, you might say, "Fantastic! I look forward to your endorsement of my promotion at the senior table." If they are curious or disagree, see if you can get to their specific point of disagreement and respond to that. If they say nothing, say, "Let me tell you why I am so confident in this idea." When they arrive at agreement, ask them to do something that demonstrates they are aligned with your thinking.

When this interaction is over, you're ready to enter the final stage of the STAR model, *Review*.

Ask yourself:

- Did I act in a way that was aligned with my values?
- Does this situation need to be brought to the attention of others? Your boss, HR, a health and safety leader, the police.
- Do I have an opportunity to learn from this interaction through debriefing it with a peer or mentor?

Much of this is likely new to you. As with any new skill, it takes practice to become great at it. The key is to remember that you cannot only survive sticky situations, but you can also emerge being seen as a leader. One who was calm, intentional, confident, and inspiring. These situations happen every day, and it can feel like you're receiving, reacting, or "dealing with" sticky situations, but I want you to remember that it's still all you. By using the STAR model, you still have the power.

CHAPTER 7

Kraft Dinner

I love Kraft Dinner. Always have. For me, it's comfy food. It must be the case that it taps into a feeling or memory of safety, security, being taken care of. It *must* be that, because it sure as hell isn't the mind-blowing flavour, the nutrient-packed ingredients, or the way it makes me feel after eating it. Yes, I was served Kraft Dinner by my mom when I was young, and continued eating it—well, I still eat it, at least four times a year. For you, maybe it's tomato soup or grilled cheese sandwiches. There's just something about the food we were served as kids. While our palettes have certainly progressed past Kraft Dinner, it's still my comfy food. Other brands have come along and aimed to replace my Kraft Dinner. Healthier boxes, maybe they use a rice noodle or organic pasta. But when I need Kraft Dinner, nothing else will do.

Don't worry, this isn't actually an entire chapter on Kraft Dinner or why I love it. It's about comfy food in general and why we love it. It's the perfect parallel to our contentment in the known, the tried and true, the status quo, the comfort zone. There's an old saying in neuroscience: "Neurons that fire together, wire together." This means the more you run a neural circuit in your brain, the stronger that circuit becomes. This explains why we gravitate to the same food, listen to the same songs, and travel the same routes. And what's so wrong with comfort and contentment? Why must I aim to disrupt what works? Well, beyond the obvious downsides of Kraft Dinner (lack of nutrients, minerals, and vitamins), if it was the only thing I ate, I'd certainly be missing out on other wonderful food, new flavours, cultural experiences, and the opportunity to discover new things about myself through food. Plus, I like grocery shopping.

From trying new food, to changing seasons, to adapting to new technology, to changes in our family makeup, change impacts all areas of our lives. Because of this, being able to successfully adapt to change will help ensure greater personal and professional success.

Most people have a negative reaction to change. They don't welcome it; they are fearful of it, and some even intentionally avoid it. Why are so many people uncomfortable with change? There are several factors that can make change difficult. First, was the change your idea or one that was imposed on you? I mean, was the pink hair you left the salon with your idea or a mistake by your hair stylist? If it was your idea, it was a change that you were happy with, maybe even proud of. If it wasn't your idea, that pink hair might take some getting used to. Second, was the change something you planned for, or was it unplanned? Did you move houses because you decided you wanted a new neighbourhood or bigger space, or did you move because your previous house burned to the ground? If it was your decision, you had time to pack, declutter, organize, and take your time selecting your new home. If it was the result of a catastrophe, you likely found yourself dealing with feelings of grief, taking stock of what you've lost/need to replace, and scrambling to find a new home. Third, is the change something you were prepared for? Did you have time to consider what you will need to be successful at this change? Or is the other side of this change unknown? Did you move your desk to the third floor after you had time to think about the benefits, visit your colleagues, and scope out the kitchen on that floor? Or did you show up to work one day and find that your desk had been moved for you? This is about whether you had the time, skills, coping mechanisms, and reinforcement needed in place before the change occurred to face the change with confidence. When you own the decision to make a change, you are better able to handle the change itself. Here's why...

Oftentimes, when facing change, we're really dealing with the emotion of fear. Fear of what life will look like after the change. Fear of the unknown. Fear of failure—what if I don't look good with pink hair? What if I don't find a suitable new house? What if I don't click with my colleagues on the third floor? In each of these anxiety-ridden thoughts, we're struggling with insecurity, a challenge for our ego. In some cases, it may be the imposter syndrome. Many of us are consumed by the need for validation, from others and ourselves. We don't want others to judge us and think that we don't measure up, and we don't want to do things we won't be good at. Our poor little egos can't manage it.

Don't limit yourself to areas that you know and are familiar with, as you will never have the opportunity to grow and enhance your skillset if you stick with jobs and responsibilities you have already done repeatedly.

Most people who say they don't like change are likely recalling a negative change event that included one or more of the above factors: the change was imposed, unplanned, or you felt unprepared. Yet, those aren't the only kinds of changes. What about positive change events? Here's a few to get your mind going: having a baby; getting promoted; taking a vacation; welcoming a new pet; mastering a new recipe; winning new business; meeting a new friend; completing a program. Stop now and think of three positive change events that you've experienced within the last six months. See? Change can be good and feel good.

What I'd like to do is help you develop appreciation for the change itself, not only the result or outcome of the change. Positive outcome or not, change is a good thing. Here's how.

Change is a powerful coach. There is very little else in this world that can improve our adaptability like change. Frequent change makes us better at adapting to new environments, new people, and new situations.

Imagine if you could somehow (although I'm not sure it's possible) completely avoid change. You found a routine for all you do and stuck to it. What would your life look like? What would those limitations be blocking for you? What experiences would you miss out on? Without change, improvements don't happen, we become stagnant. You might think that this avoidance of change would create a safe environment for you—one where you can count on things being as they are. Again, we know this is an impossible reality, but if it was possible, I guarantee that your life would be gray, boring, repetitive, unfulfilling, and void of joy. Safe? Yes, but what is safety worth? What is the trade-off?

Another benefit of change is that it can spark excitement in your personal and professional life. When you are open to change, you broaden your perspective, seek newness, look through windows that otherwise can't be seen, and discover pockets of joy. Have you ever travelled to a place that introduced you to something new? Maybe it was hearing a new language spoken by locals, or swimming in water that was a colour you've never seen. Perhaps it was visiting a historic site that taught you something new about a region's traditions.

I'm sure you'll agree, those experiences can only happen when you change your environment, leave your comfy, safe home, and courageously invite change.

It is only with change that new beginnings and new opportunities are realized. Some of you might be thinking, "Yeah but I really like my life exactly as it is right now." Good for you! That's absolutely fabulous; you've created a life that brings you joy and contentment, and clearly you are grateful for it. Now, reflect on how you got there. I assure you, your path was filled with a ton of changes along the way. Likely decision points that altered your course. Maybe you moved, had a family, travelled, went to school, met new friends and mentors. I can't say exactly what your pivot points were, but I can say with confidence that there were many. My question is, if we accept the premise that joy is limitless, why stop now? Yes, be grateful for where you are and what you have now, but don't quit. Continue to invite newness and watch your life grow.

Change is normal and something we experience every day. A plan with your friend falls through, you head to the gym only to discover it's closed, the skirt you wanted to wear has a massive stain on it (this happened to me yesterday)—all these changes are small in nature and perhaps insignificant, but they require us to pivot, adapt. We don't always look forward to change, but remember that every time change happens, you have an opportunity to grow, learn, and develop new skills. When your friend ditched you, maybe you used that time to sit in a park and read a book that taught you something (like this one). When the gym was closed, maybe you decided to go for a run instead and discovered a new neighbourhood gem. And when your skirt was stained, maybe you went shopping for something new (or, in my case, located the nearest dry cleaner). From the day you were born, your life has been a series of changes and reactions to change. When you stop to reflect on this, you will realize you are quite experienced at managing change. Every single change is an invitation to grow.

What about big changes? They are the scary ones. One might even say life-changing. I'd say these changes present an even greater opportunity for growth. I'm sure you've heard of the word *resilience*. Since I'm going to talk about it here, let's begin by defining it so we're all on the same page. According to the Webster's dictionary, resilience is "an ability to recover from or adjust easily to misfortune or change." I've noticed that when people are speaking about someone being resilient, it's generally cited as a positive trait. "She's so resilient." I mean, that's a compliment, right? I'd want someone to say that about me, and they do. So, how does one become resilient? The answer lies in the definition. You can see when you reread the definition that for resilience to be present, there is a requirement of "misfortune or change." That is to say that one cannot be, or become resilient, without experiencing change. When you transition through a tough change, you often emerge stronger, more resilient, and more resourceful. The reverse is also true: if you protect yourself from change, you'll be less resilient when the big changes come, and they will. The fact is, like anything, the more we are exposed to and practiced at navigating change, the better we are at it. People who go through the most change are the best at it. They've built up their resilience—the ability of that muscle to do what it is meant to do, regardless of the circumstance. Like you, I've had many changes in my life. In fact, I've had quite a few significant life events. I've moved across the country four times, I've been married and divorced twice, I've started my own company (and wrote a book!), I've raised a beautiful dog, I've changed careers, I've lost my father, and my mother is living with advanced Alzheimer's disease. You can see why some call me resilient. Many of these changes were unwelcomed, but all have made me who I am today. Like it or not, I wouldn't be where I am or who I am today without these changes. The more change we endure, the easier it becomes. Even imposed, unplanned, and unprepared change.

Perhaps my favourite benefit of going through change is that every time you do, you're collecting proof that it's not so scary, that you can do it. You're gaining the courage to face change and the confidence that you will be ok on the other side.

One of the best ways to be more comfortable with change is to focus on its benefits. Whenever we are faced with change in our personal or professional lives, remember these benefits. So, let's look at the starting points for moving beyond the comfort, and yes, I'm going to use another Kraft Dinner story. My friend's daughter liked to eat *only* Kraft Dinner. Nothing else would do. My friend naturally became concerned about how to broaden her daughter's taste. She thought to do it in baby steps. She didn't remove the Kraft Dinner; she added to it. First, with peas. Then, with peas and carrots. It took a while, but eventually that little girl began to love peas and carrots. Moral of the story—when you can, baby-step it.

Now, in this example, the decision to move out of comfort and towards something new and unknown was determined by my friend, the mother. As an adult, in most cases you're the one who needs to make that decision.

I'm going to show you how to lead yourself through change. Of course, the same rules apply to leading others through change, but as you read, I encourage you to think about *you*—changes that you've been through, are thinking of making, and the changes you are in right now.

The first step in making a change is for you to be aware of the need for change. You've likely picked up on the fact that I'm a confident woman. So confident, in fact, that I had a blind spot to one of my weaknesses. When I was in my twenties, I was walking along a sidewalk on my way to a doctor's appointment for my annual physical when I caught my reflection in the glass of a storefront. I was like, *"Yes, girl! Lookin' fine!"* Feeling like a million bucks, I walked into my doctor's office. She was a straight shooter; one might say she lacked some bedside manner; however, perhaps for this reason, she was just the doctor I needed. We started a conversation, covering the basics of lifestyle (exercise, smoking, diet, drinking, family medical history, stress levels, etc.). Then she said, "OK, hop on the scale." I did and didn't take note of the number. But she did. I stepped off, and she said, "OK, I'm going to send you for blood work, and included in that will be a cholesterol check, which you get for free, because you hit so many high-risk categories for heart disease." This made me curious. High risk? She explained that my family has a history of heart disease, I was relatively inactive, and I was overweight. Huh? I was overweight? Now, before we go any further, I must tell you that, at this point, I hadn't weighed myself since I was a strong, slim, fit lifeguard and about 18 years old, so I really had no idea what the numbers on a scale meant or what my weight was. All I knew was that I felt okay and looked amazing. She said, "Yes, overweight. You're 175 pounds." Medically, that was overweight for my height, so regardless of how good I felt and looked, my body was not healthy. I said, "Wait a second, I weigh so much that I qualify to get medical testing done for free?!" She nodded her head. If that wasn't enough to give me a wake-up call, her phone call to me a few days later confirming that I did have high cholesterol certainly was. That was when my awareness of the need to change was established.

I was given the option to avoid medication and try my best to lower my cholesterol through improved diet and exercise. Here comes the next step in making a change—desire. Like setting goals for yourself, making the decision to change something works best when you actually *want* to change. This new lifestyle was going to see me make less trips to McDonalds and more trips to the gym. I was not particularly excited about this. While my awareness of the need to change was high, my desire was not. I liked my life! Yummy (crappy) food, relaxing nights on the couch. What would I even *do* at a gym? Was I going to have to stop eating cheese? Ugh—I was not excited about this new "lifestyle." Here's where many people get stuck when making a change. It's possible that their desire may be low because of the unknown of what their life will look like after the change. This is fear. My desire to be healthier and feel better was definitely high, but the fear of all of the unknown components of this new lifestyle was choking my enthusiasm.

In the wise words of my sister, "People do what they want to do, and they don't do what they don't want to do." We make time for that which we desire. If you don't want to go to the gym today, I'm confident that you will find as many ways as necessary to avoid going. Laundry, walk the dog, organize your spices—anything will do! Very little else is as effective as we ourselves are at creating roadblocks to participating in activities for which we have a low desire. In order to get out of your own way, you must increase your desire.

One way to get unstuck if your desire is low due to fear of the unknown is to take action. We can sit in place and think all we want. We can think ourselves into and out of just about anything, given enough time. Have you ever heard the saying "analysis paralysis"? Overthinking can block us from making change because it can stop or limit action. Remember my friend putting peas in Kraft Dinner? Change, especially big change, may require baby steps. My best advice is do *something*—take a step, a baby step at first, but do something. My first action was I went to the community centre down the street and walked through the door. Seems like no big deal; I'm sure that little action didn't, in itself, lower my cholesterol, but what it did do was unlock a series of subsequent actions that did. Next, I bought a three-month membership (I wasn't ready to commit to anything longer) and basically walked around like an imposter. Avoiding the machines, I lingered around the bulletin boards in the hallway and saw a schedule that showed "Kickboxing, Tues/Thurs 6:30–7:30 p.m. with Nancy." I looked at my watch; it was 6:25 p.m. and it was Thursday. Serendipitous, perhaps. I liked Nancy. This wasn't a boppy aerobics class; Nancy was the real deal. She had the ability to knock me into next week if she wanted to. I had so much fun at this first class that I vowed to attend every Tuesday and Thursday. After about a month, I had made new friends and felt myself getting stronger. Not to mention the free high I was getting from increased levels of dopamine, noradrenaline, and serotonin—the perfect brain smoothie. This was reinforcement enough for me to continue, and I did for several months. Everything was getting easier. I decided to augment my fitness regime with a few gym sessions, and one Wednesday night, when I was walking by the room I normally had kickboxing in, I heard really loud, high-energy, fun music playing. I looked in and saw two hot guys training people in something, and I wanted to be part of whatever that something was. The music was by the Black Eyed Peas, and the sport was boxing. Here is exactly when my desire to adopt a healthier lifestyle was established. Thus began my journey to health.

OK, so now I know I need to make some changes, and I'm motivated to do so. The next question is whether I have the knowledge needed to be successful. I had to learn things like what food helps or worsens cholesterol and how to grocery shop for healthy food. Once I'd learned these things, I needed to make sure that I had the skills to make the change. I had to learn how to cook a bunch of new healthy recipes. Do you know how to roast a vegetable or grill fish? It's OK if you don't know how to do these things; I'm sure you have many talents. The message here is that you need to have the knowledge and ability in order for the change to stick.

Finally, you must put something in place to keep up the new behaviour. For me, I made the leap and committed to an annual gym membership and decided that every Sunday would be meal prep day. These accountabilities set me up for long-term success. For some, stars on a chart on your fridge might do the trick, or recruiting a workout buddy. Systems that hold you accountable. We're developing new habits, and that requires consistency.

Change is hard work.

When I was 45, I completely started my life over again. And, no, I'm not being dramatic. The years prior saw me lose my father, settle my mother into a long-term care facility, sell my house and everything in it, and once again relocate to a different province. I was moving into a friend's fully furnished apartment, so I'd done the math on whether I should ship and store my belongings or just repurchase it all when the time comes. The math said to sell/donate it all. I arrived at my new place with my dog, my father's guitar, and a few cherished pieces of art. I didn't even own cutlery. I had to believe in myself that I would be OK. More than okay; successful. I had to have the confidence that I could do it. The change was underway, and doubting myself would have derailed future opportunities. The way I saw it was that if I didn't have confidence in myself to make this move, what is the alternative? We have a decision to make every time we face change. Do we want to embrace it and charge toward it with confidence, or will we let it scare us and have it rock our confidence? There are no certainties in how things will turn out during or following change. No guarantees that it'll be easy or that the grass will be any greener. This uncertainty is part of the package of change. Rather than let that scare you, let it thrill you. There is growth in discomfort.

When I worked with street kids in Vancouver, we'd only have them for a short time before they took off for other things, things like drugs or prostitution, so our time together was very valuable and had to be used wisely. Here is when I learned of the transtheoretical model of change *developed by Prochaska and DiClemente*. Most models of change talk about progression—moving through change, adapting to it. But the practicality of this model with this population was incredible. The neat thing about this model is that it helped me easily identify where someone was in the process and then introduce the best intervention. Here's what I mean: if a youth was only *thinking* about recovery, it would be too soon to bring them to a detox facility. But if they had reviewed a few pamphlets and tied up loose ends, it would be an ideal time to do so. You can see how this model helped me maximize the impact I could make in little time with the youth.

Much in the same way, you can use this model to support yourself through change. The original model has six stages of change and I've expanded on each and included a seventh stage. They are:

Precontemplation. In this stage, you lack awareness of the need to change. Without awareness, there will be no change. Remember when I went to the doctor and abruptly increased my awareness of the need to get healthier? I can assure you that as I blissfully walked (pretty much danced) into my doctor's office, I would have never even conceived of the idea of cutting out mayo and hitting the gym. That's why you can think of this stage as the catalyst of all change. Step one is knowing that a change needs to happen. How can you move through this stage? Increase your openness; seek to learn new things—about the world, about others, and most importantly, about yourself.

Contemplation. Consider this the "I'm just thinking about it" stage. Here, your awareness of the need to change has been established, but your desire may be low. Therefore, your commitment to change is also low. When you find yourself in this stage, your best course of action is to not act at all. Sit in it, consider all of the options, consider every side, work hard to sell yourself every possibility. It is imperative that you stay in contemplation until you land squarely on the decision to embrace this change or not. The alternative, which many people do, is to push yourself into action when you're not yet sold on the change. I'd say this is the number one reason people drop out of change. As you deliberate, gather all of the available information. Do your research; maybe even talk to others who have gone through the change. Begin to imagine your life during and after the change. Lots to think about.

Preparation. Your mind is made up; you've decided the change will happen! Now, you're in the "getting ready" stage. What I love about this stage is that it highlights the importance of setting yourself up for success. If you decide to begin a new job search tomorrow morning at nine but then realize at 9 a.m. that you don't have a resume, you will most certainly fail at your attempt at changing your employment status. If you decide you're going to hit up a spin class tonight and just show up at the studio at six without checking the schedule, you may be disappointed, having not first checked the schedule. Deciding to eat healthier and beginning with a healthy dinner without first buying the ingredients will leave you hungry and working with what you do have in the fridge (which may not be healthy). OK, you get my drift.

Action. The thinking and planning are over; it's time to get it done! This is observable behaviour, like going to the gym, making a meal, applying for a job. When you find yourself here, remember my earlier advice of baby-stepping it. Any action is action, regardless of how big the splash. Be kind to yourself here, and pause to recognize and celebrate your accomplishment, even if it was something small like walking around the block or applying for one job.

Maintenance. This stage is about making the new behaviour stick. A common mistake people often make is to think that no additional work is needed here. The reality is that something new does need to be introduced to reinforce the behaviour. When I was young, my mom would put a chart on the fridge and place stars on the days when I did what she wanted. After her measures of success were achieved (a week of not peeing the bed), I'd get a small reward. This is the essence of reinforcement. Other examples of this could be recruiting an accountability buddy—someone who tracks your new behaviour, or, even better, joins you in the new behaviour. I have a friend who I know is expecting me to show up for spin classes. I also get dinged $25 if I miss a class. These are reinforcement measures which help make the new behaviour a habit, or normalized behaviour.

Relapse. Not all new behaviours stick the first time. In fact, it is very common for us to revert back to our old behaviour. The reason for this is that the old behaviour is well-learned, well-practiced, deeply engrained, and comfortable. However, a reframe I like to put on this stage is that if the relapse advances your understanding of the upside of the new behaviour, and/or reinforces your desire for change, it is called a *prolapse*. Be careful not to throw away all of your hard effort and small wins along the way because of a slip. When I decided to improve my eating habits, I was on a good run. I'd maintained a healthy diet for months. Then, one morning, I was tired and feeling lazy after a night of too much wine. I woke up to a craving a McDonald's breakfast, so I got myself an Egg McMuffin and a hashbrown and loved every bite. Later that day, my tummy was a mess, and I felt like crap. I knew right away that my body was unhappy with my decision. That yucky feeling stayed with me and reminded me that the immediate gratification was not worth the cost of sabotaging my new healthy lifestyle. I definitely learned from it. Yes, I still succumb to my impulses from time to time, but I don't let it take me down. I don't assign the slips as complete failures, but rather get back onto my program as soon as possible.

Termination. There is a stage when the change is considered to be complete, and this is it. Here, there is no temptation to revert to your previous behaviour. Your new behaviour is the new normal. It becomes the new comfy food.

It's important for you to remember that moving through every stage is progress, and each micro-win deserves celebration and a flaunt. Tell your friends and family how you're doing and feel proud of all you've achieved throughout this change.

Some final thoughts on embracing change to close this chapter for you—

Be **brave**. Even though some people may be uncomfortable with your confidence or flaunts, do your best to overcome your inclination to hide and play it safe. I've heard members from many minority groups talk about having an aversion to risk because they can't afford the loss, politically, should they "get it wrong." But you will never always get it right. It's true that everyone feels better when we know our stuff, are well prepared, and have achieved subject mastery. However, change brings newness, and newness requires new learning. It's said that, on average, with each new role you take, there will be a six-month learning curve. In this unsteady time, when your legs are still wobbly, say what you do know with confidence. Share your ideas and be okay with learning as you go. No one has all of the answers. For those of you who do take chance in the face of uncertainty, you will be rewarded; after all, the saying is *high risk, high reward.*

I called this point "be brave" rather than "have courage" because bravery is doing something in the presence of real fear. I know that the fear some of you may feel in projecting confidence in high-risk situations is real. A wise friend once told me that her life mantra is "Face the fear and do it anyway." It's a good one, and that's what I'm asking you to do.

Make **positive assumptions**. The fact is that most people want you to win, want you to succeed. We like victory more than loss, even when it comes to others. Generally speaking, our audiences are friendly audiences. From my experience, one of the main reasons people are so afraid of public speaking is that they fear judgement. But when I take the stage, I always assume the audience is quietly (sometimes loudly!) cheering me on. They don't want my slides to not work or my mic to cut out. Think about this: when you watch figure skating on TV, or any other sport for that matter, do you really want to see them fall? *No!* It's so painful to watch them fall after all the hard work they've put into their training. The same spectator attitude exists when you're performing. For this reason, I encourage you to think positively. We get to choose the direction we look. We get to choose what we focus on. If I assume I'm going to choke on that stage, I likely will. If I assume that others are keen to hear what I have to say and that I'll rock it, I likely will. Perception is reality.

Be entirely **selfish**. There will be changes placed upon you that you have a low desire to make. Changes that others have decided for you. In those instances, seek to draw the value and/or learning.

There is always something to be gained, even if it's not obvious in the short term. Perhaps your desk was moved to another floor, and you really liked your old spot. Well, begin looking for the silver lining. Maybe your new spot is closer to the kitchen! It definitely presents you with an opportunity to make new work friends. Perhaps being on this new floor brings you closer to the sales team, which allows you to learn about a new part of the business. Finally, in these forced changes, focus on that which you can control. I'll always give people time to grieve what has been lost, but it's also super-important to move beyond that so your new learning can emerge.

Tap into your key **relationships.** Many changes, big and small, are better navigated with support. It's not a weakness to recruit others to help you adapt to change. The most senior leaders I've ever met have a list of people they lean on, personally and professionally. You don't have to go it alone. Surround yourself with people who will be your champions, catch you if you fall, and help you spot and mitigate risks.

Finally, remember: when you want to change, you're **incredible** at doing it.

Go forth and welcome change into your life. You never know; there could be gourmet mac and cheese that pairs nicely with a glass of wine right around the corner.

CHAPTER 8

Helpful Advice

I'm often asked for advice on how to navigate big challenges and nuanced situations—many of which were already covered in this book. I'm told that my suggestions are helpful, which makes me think: what *is* helpful advice, and why is it so rare?

To me, helpful advice is two things: (1) it makes sense, and (2) it is actionable in ways that it ultimately leads to a desired outcome. This chapter aspires to be both of these things. But to do so, I must begin by helping you to identify *un*helpful advice.

Let's start with a simple example. A friend has been laid off and is looking for support to secure employment.

Unhelpful advice: You should apply to everything.

Helpful advice: What's worked for me are these four things: (1) seek professional help to polish up your resume; (2) define your must-haves and nice-to-haves; (3) identify companies who you'd like to work for and are offering opportunities that align with your needs; and (4) do your homework then reach out to each company, whether they're actively hiring or not.

Note the difference between the two offerings of advice. In the helpful one, each step begins with a verb, thereby giving your friend real actions they can take that will lead them to meaningful employment. The steps are doable, and most importantly, if executed, will position them for success.

This may be unpopular, but I put vision boards and manifesting in the unhelpful camp. I know. We hear a lot about the power of visualizing our hopes and dreams, and don't get me wrong, I do think it's valuable to be clear about your goals. However, I don't see these acts as things that will get you promoted or advance your career in other ways. Manifesting might be powerful, but it's too long a dotted line to attribute causality to the outcomes it claims to produce. It can act as a centering beacon, but it isn't tactical enough to be the foundation of a plan that leads to results.

The bad news continues. Platitudes, also known as empty expressions, are commonly heard at every leadership conference, especially those geared toward women. It's as though *actual* helpful advice is intentionally withheld. Platitudes find themselves in the unhelpful camp because they are mostly focused on *what* you should do, or the attitude with which you should do it, rather than detailing exactly *how* you're supposed to do it.

It's time to demystify those platitudes, break them down, and make them actionable.

Platitude: "Say yes to everything."
I am quite sure that you are all busy enough and that saying yes to everything is terrible advice. The genesis of this platitude is that we should be open to change, open to new ideas, and thereby avail ourselves to new opportunities. I was once told that the more projects I "get to" work on, the more people I'll be able to interact with and impress, which will lead to more learning and ultimately advance my career. But taken literally, this advice would see us lose ourselves to

long hours and exhaustion, which would lead to lower overall productivity or poorer quality of work and thinner relationships—at work and at home. Terrible advice. If it's meant to inspire us to be open to change, then say that.

Helpful advice: "Be strategic in choosing opportunities that increase your visibility."
You can't say yes to everything, and there is power in saying no. The neat thing is, you can only say yes or no to something—not both. So, every time you're saying yes to something, you're saying no to something else, and vice versa. In fact, a colleague of mine, Dan Dumsha, often focuses on what he's saying yes to when saying no to others. For example, if I invited him for dinner and he was already committed to spending time with his parents, he'd say, "I'm spending tonight with Mom and Dad. Let's plan for another night." You see, the emphasis of his response is to communicate his priority and what he's saying yes to. In this instance, his yes is more meaningful, more important than the reasoning behind the no. The explanation fits better with what he's saying yes to.

Not all opportunities were created equally, so you must get choosy about what you're saying yes to. Attend a conference with your boss? Yes. Take notes for a meeting where you aren't a contributor? No. Head up the Safety Committee to get more time with your next leader? Yes.

Assess the opportunity using a gains perspective. This idea was introduced in the "After Hours" chapter, where I encouraged you to evaluate opportunities through the lens of benefit to you. It's ok to be selfish; no one else is waking up every day wondering how they can advance your career.

Platitude: "Seize every opportunity that comes your way."

I've heard this one at just about every women's event I've ever attended. And I chuckle in disbelief that this is the best we can do to support the next generation of women leaders. I mean, first, where *are* all of these opportunities I'm supposed to be seizing?! Are they locked away in a closet? Am I walking down the wrong halls? Are they flying over my head? This platitude implies that opportunities are abound and all we have to do is stick out our hand and grab them. Like snowflakes.

Secondly, are we to assume that *every* opportunity will be a great fit for our skills, passions, and career aspirations? That seems a bit utopian. We need to remember that we have the power and ability to make decisions about what's right for us. Not every job offer, role, relocation, or project is right for us. Be discerning.

Helpful advice: "Create the opportunities you seek."

The last two jobs I had didn't exist before I came along. But I knew what I wanted, and I used my skills to make it happen. I considered the business case for my proposed new role; after all, I had to be compelling. I used my communication skills to inspire the bosses to see the potential gains as I did. I used my negotiation skills to create a win-win proposition. And I used my relationship-building skills to create rapport and establish trust. It's this kind of articulated advice that can truly help others discover opportunities. Also, isn't it terribly empowering to think that you can have anything you want? All you have to do is design the plan to get there and make it happen. It is, though, more than simply sticking my hand in the air to grab mystical opportunities.

Platitude: "Find a mentor."

I've talked about various relationships in other chapters, but it's worth repeating. A mentor is a committed ear who can guide you by sharing their experience and knowledge with you. Helpful, yes. But many women don't know how to execute on this platitude. *How* do I find a mentor? What should I be looking for in a mentor? How does the relationship work? Maybe I already have one and don't know it? How can I get the most from my mentor? And what's this about a sponsor?

Helpful advice: "Build strategic relationships."
My main issue with the generic advice about finding a mentor is that it overemphasizes the importance of mentors. Look, no one does it alone—we all have supporters, cheerleaders, allies, champions. But I do also know many successful people who have never had a formal, official mentor. So, if you don't have one right now, don't stress about it! Mentors are great, and I talked about mine in an earlier chapter, but we require a good mix of people to support us. If any one role should be singled out and overemphasized when speaking to emerging leaders, it should be a sponsor.

I'd say my early success was strongly due to the fact that I spent much of my energy (aside from actually doing the work I was being paid to do) building solid relationships internally with those who could help me advance (a.k.a., sponsors). External guidance is nice and important, but building direct-line relationships with those in power can't be beat.

Platitude: "Take control of your career."
But *how*? I don't know where I want to go or if I'm even qualified. I don't know if now is a good time to ask my boss about this new role. I feel like I should just be thankful for the job I have today. Oh yes, I plan to talk to my boss about this in my performance review.

Helpful advice: "Set career goals."

This is an area where men are winning. They know the *how*. Here's what they do: They determine the role they want, they clearly and **unapologetically** articulate career goals to people who have the power to make it happen, and then they insist on co-creating a professional development plan that sees them in that role within a set timeframe. Oh, and then they hold everyone accountable to that plan and timeframe.

Platitude: "Advice to my 20-year-old self."

I know. This one really is meant to be helpful. Successful leaders sharing what they learned along the way in hopes of saving you the pains of their earlier mistakes or weaknesses. It's kind. The problem is that hindsight is always 20/20, and our 20-year-old selves are not equipped to navigate the world like a more seasoned professional. We might not even be ready to hear about your insightful lessons learned. So don't expect us to! We're going to make mistakes as we learn, just like you did, and we'll learn invaluable lessons from those mistakes because they were ours.

The seasoned leader didn't get it right the first time when they were younger, likely because they didn't know what they should do or, more likely, how to do it. Often, it was the courage or confidence they were lacking at the time. That's why hearing successful women tell younger women that if they could do it all again, they'd have "been kinder to themselves" or "been less afraid" is not helpful. I mean, we all know we should be less afraid, but HOW!!?

Helpful advice: "You're doing great."

Learning from other people's life lessons isn't nearly as impactful as making them yourself. You have to trip and fall. You have to get it wrong. We need experiences of winning and losing to gain confidence and lessen our fears. It's also a fact that failing isn't avoidable.

Just like good advice, cautionary advice can be bad advice. What works and doesn't work for one person isn't necessarily true for another. I've been told to avoid roles that require too much travel because it interferes with work-life balance. I've been told not to become too specialized in my skills so that I keep my options open. And I've been told that writing a book is difficult and thankless. All of this advice didn't suit me, and thankfully I knew that.

Pave your own path. It might be bumpy, twisty, and challenging for you, but it was for our predecessors as well.

My final caution on unhelpful advice is that even the best, seemingly most helpful advice can be bad when it comes from a source who has ulterior motives. Be aware of who is advising you, what their advice is, and where it is coming from. For example, a colleague who tells you that you talk too much at meetings might be trying to quiet you to increase their own political capital by making space for more of their ideas or at the very least lessening the threat that you present to them. Feedback is a gift that you can choose to accept or not. Apply your political savviness and decide what works best for you.

Simply put, watch who you take your coaching notes from.

I've reviewed what I consider unhelpful advice. Now for the fun part. Here are my top 10 tips, which are truly helpful advice.

1. Become a positive thinker.

There's a lot to be negative about in life. Life is complex and can be overwhelming. With all of the reinforcing external cues (e.g., negative "click-bait" media), it can be difficult to recognize how much is within your control. Perhaps this is why most people are negative thinkers (and speakers). But there are also a lot of good, positive things in life. So, what other reasons lead us to live in a culture of negativity? I have a few theories.

First, for some, it takes effort. If you are inherently a negative thinker, it can require a good amount of energy to go against what seems more natural. It might feel more familiar to think this way, while overcoming negativity requires us to sit with and work through discomfort. It can be much easier to fall into a negative rumination cycle.

Second, some of us would rather have low or no expectations now than be disappointed later. A negative outlook can act as protection. We see this in people who have their "walls up" as a defensive measure. One might say that our tendency to focus on the negative is our survival instinct at work.

Finally, it's not "cool." It's common to hear people speaking negatively, complaining, venting. In this way, speaking positively can be seen as going against social norms and expectations.

Have no fear; I have at least that many counterarguments in favour of positive thinking.

I very much believe that there is at least as much good in the world as there is bad, and we will all be better served by focusing on it. It is essential that you understand that, for the most part, you have control over your thoughts. And that like channel surfing, you can surf until you land on something that is positive. It is a choice.

Consider the links among your thoughts, emotions, decisions, and behaviours. We all have thoughts that stimulate feelings. Together, they will lead us to deciding what action we will do, or not do. This is a strong link and explains the notion of the self-fulfilling prophecy. I'm sure you've heard the expression "Whether you think it will work or not, you're right." Our thoughts control everything that is within our control. Our thoughts influence our emotions, and vice versa. And ultimately, our thoughts lead to our reality.

There are tremendous benefits of focusing on the positive, owning your power, and taking control. Our brain plays a larger role in our emotions, decisions, and behaviours than we give it credit for. Of course, there are things beyond our control, but you can influence a lot more than you may realize.

Engage your brain/mind to help you achieve the things you most desire.

Take back your power and use your brilliant mind to set you on the course you desire.

2. Make positive assumptions.

What is the most generous interpretation of the intentions, words, and actions you can make about yourself and others? Search for it. It might not come to you inherently; this might be an area where you have to train your brain. And why should you? Well, let me ask you this: If someone saw you walking down the street at 6 a.m., would you want them to assume you're coming home late from a big night out? Or would you want them to assume you're out for your morning walk, getting the day started on the right foot? This really goes back to being kind, a true golden rule of humanity.

I have a few friends who've been jaded by the local dating scene, and because of it, they see prospects first through a skeptical, cynical lens. "He's probably married and looking to cheat on his wife." "She's probably a gold digger." I online dated for a couple of years, and my empirical evidence tells me that these "probability" statements are simply unfounded. All people who are "out there" are looking for a connection. Yes, some are slime balls, but in my experience, most were people like me—good folks looking for love.

The question is, if we'd like others to make kind assumptions about us, why don't we do the same for others?

Assuming you're convinced, let's talk about how to train your brain to make positive assumptions. I used to take a commuter ferry across an inlet to get to work and back every day. To increase my positive mindset, I'd play a little game with myself. I'd look around and spot a person or group, and I'd challenge myself to create a story about who I was observing. Before I go any further, let me point out that we all already do this—make up stories about others. It's just usually "judgey" and not at all kind. The real challenge here is to make up stories about others that are gracious, kind, and perhaps even flattering.

On my way home from work one evening, I spotted a woman with three children who were running around the ferry like they'd just eaten a pound of sugar. To the negative observer, it would appear she "had no control over those children" or, at best, "was a desperate single mom who needs help." In my mind, my story was that she was quite a brilliant woman who knew she had 12 minutes (that's how long the ferry was) to burn the day's energy out of these kids. She knew it was safe for them to be moving about, and she didn't feel the need to contain them. They were having fun, they were safe, they even met other passengers and made them smile with their shenanigans. An all-star mom.

With this personal exercise in mind, I challenged my single friends to engage in a similar exercise. We were on vacation in Florida, driving to breakfast, when I asked them both to tell me a positive assumption about every person who was walking on the sidewalk as we drove past. It worked. And the best part was watching how these positive, made-up stories made them feel. I could see it in their smiles and hear it in their voices. You see, making positive assumptions about others contributes to your wellbeing.

Very convincing, I know.

Notice what you're focusing on.

Choose to see the good. In yourself. In others.

Celebrate wins. Give attention to positive outcomes.

3. Build positive habits and pivot as needed.

Our brain is here to help us succeed. Let's face it: generally, we're lazy creatures. Most of us prefer the easy route, the known, the predictable. As we talked about in the chapter "Kraft Dinner," there's comfort in the known. So, let's use that to our advantage by establishing routines that set us up for success.

I always say a great day starts the night before. Sleep is when our bodies and minds rejuvenate, heal, and restore. If getting a good night's sleep is a challenge for you, work on that. Your nightly routine is a good place to start. I try not to eat or exercise three hours before bed; it's how I signal to my body that its work is done for the day and rest is coming. I also do not sleep with my phone in my bedroom. It stays in the kitchen, plugged in, waiting for me the next day. It also gets a break. And this way, when I roll over, I'm not tempted to scroll through social media or read work emails. Everything can wait until you wake up. I promise. You've earned the night off; take it. If sleep is a serious issue for you, I encourage you to speak with your doctor about it.

In the morning, establish a wake-up routine that works for you. I do five things every morning before I look at my phone: pee, wash my face, brush my teeth, take my medication, and make a coffee. It's OK to be selfish and keep those precious first 15 minutes to yourself. Everything can wait. I like to move my body in the morning, either with a spin class or a morning walk with my dog and girlfriends. I find that gives me the energy I need to get me through the day. And finally, before I sit down to work, I set my intentions for the day. This starts with checking in with my attitude, thoughts, and mood. How am I feeling? What do I want to achieve today? Then I set realistic goals for that day. Realistic means achievable. And achieving those goals = flaunts. For a goal to be achievable, it has to be within my ability for that given day. Some days I can accomplish more than others. Be kind to yourself by considering your capabilities each day. The days I have low energy are not the days I choose to tackle organizing my closet, managing finances, or other complex tasks. On those days, I might set a goal of reading a few chapters or finishing a few projects that might take less brainpower. I know some days we don't have full control over what we have to accomplish. You might have a job that assigns you projects, and the work must go on! Or perhaps you're a parent who simply doesn't get a day off. Even still, be gentle with yourself. Don't beat yourself up if you can't produce to expectation, we all have off days.

In the evening, I like to flaunt! Big or small, we all have achieved something by the end of every day. Remember that flaunting is not only recognizing and acknowledging your wins but also sharing them with others. Call your sis, tell your friends, or share your flaunt with your family. Everyone likes to hear good news, and if you look for it, you'll find that you always have a flaunt to share.

Finally, habits can run us into a rut. Have you ever had a routine that, after a while, wasn't serving you well? Maybe you do an activity that just doesn't excite you anymore. Let that be your signal to pivot! The gym is boring; move your fitness outside. Your walking route is predictable and no longer stimulating; change it up. Our brains like stimulation. Feed it the sights and sounds it needs to help us.

4. Be yourself.

We have an incredible need to be liked. Seen. Validated. This need can drive us to take on traits that aim to have others perceive us in a certain way, a way we believe they will like. What I've found is that what people like the most is honesty and being able to trust what they see and hear to be the truth. For better or worse, I am myself. Most, not all, people like me, and frankly, that's enough for me. I do know that it takes confidence and a good amount of self-worth to be OK with others not liking us, but you're this far into the book, and I feel like we're all there now. Give this a try. The next time you meet someone new, truly be yourself. They will appreciate the honesty. And you will find that it's easier to build real relationships with others when you're not in a disguise. It's way easier.

5. Do what your male colleagues do.

It's working.

I read somewhere that we're being told not to interrupt. I know, interrupting is not polite, and so, yes, don't make it a habit. BUT. If the communication culture at the management meetings is to boldly jump in whenever you have an idea, then you shouldn't be the only one playing by the "don't interrupt" rule. If you can't beat them, join them. The trick is, once you have them seeing you as a peer, you can be the influencer who changes that culture to one that is more conducive to listening and collaboration. But you've got to get there first.

Your male counterpart just walks into your boss's office without an official meeting planned? Do the same. We don't require special permissions that others don't.

How many of your male colleagues do you see sitting on non-value-add committees, like the social committee? Very few, if any. Be more strategic, they are. When I moved back to my hometown,

I had left as a young university grad and re-entered as a working professional. I needed to establish myself as a businesswoman, and I needed to grow my network. I considered where I might easily and quickly plug into the local business community, and it brought me to the Alumni Council of my alma mater. It just so happens that my university educated most of the local successful businesspeople of our city, so I knew it was optimal to join the council. Plus, I was looking for somewhere to add value through volunteerism. Once I joined, I learned that we were also encouraged to join a committee or two. I quickly assessed the options through a selfish gains perspective (why not?! Every committee needed volunteers, I was helping the school regardless of whether it was helping me), and I landed on the annual golf tournament. Why? Well, I saw that the sponsors and golfers from years past represented all of the big names in town, so the access to the business community would be great. Once I joined, I knew I had to figure out a way to meet as many people as possible and have them learn who I am. So, I carved out a role for myself. Emcee. For five years, I emceed that golf tournament, and all of the VIP business folks knew who I was.

Is this opportunistic? Yes. We made that a bad word. Like flaunting. Truth is, both are good for you and can be good for others.

6. Be proactive.

Perhaps you see a need for a leader in a growing area of the business. You've been tracking the momentum, watching the traction the product or service is getting, and you know it's only a matter of time before management posts the role for a division leader. Bring it to them! They will be impressed by your interest in the business, the mindfulness of the organizational needs, and your willingness to pitch the idea. It's ambitious. What's the worst that can happen?

They say no, but now see you as having a solid business acumen and drive? Not so terrible.

Don't wait to be asked; don't wait to be told; don't hesitate.

7. Own it.

Taking responsibility for anything comes with risk and reward. The more fully you embrace ownership, the higher the risk and reward. Whether you succeed or not, you've demonstrated accountability and learned something. Win-win.

I get hired by leaders all the time, asking me to help their people take on more accountability. Shying away from ownership that you've been assigned generally stems from a place of fear—what if I get it wrong? What if I don't know how to do it? What if it fails? My greatest wish would be that you quit the "what ifs" entirely. I mean, none of us have a crystal ball, and while "what ifs" might seem like sound risk management, it's also an opportunity blocker. That's right; instead, I want you to think of ownership as opportunity. What if … you get it right? What if you *do* know how to do it? What if it wins? The only way we have big wins is when we stretch, gamble, call it what you want, but owning it is the only way to show ourselves and others what we're made of.

The other issue with ownership that you might face is not wanting to be in the spotlight, taking the attention. That's why so many of us attribute our successes to the contributions of others—a trademark of the imposter syndrome. We need to get more comfortable with winning and losing and being in the spotlight regardless of the outcome.

Women tend to shy away from the spotlight more than men because we are less experienced with winning and failing. The desired outcome of two boys running on a playground is that one wins and one loses, while the desired outcome of two girls running is a tie. We also tend to participate in activities and sports that are team-based, which dilutes our ownership of winning and losing. When I work with people who shy away from failing, I coach them to do a few exercises that will set them up to fail, such as reading. Any person who reads out loud for 10 to 15 minutes straight will, inevitably, make a mistake, regardless of their reading ability. There's also an improv game I learned from my colleague, Dan Dumsha, that we play with our clients called the "S game." Two or more players co-create a story, one line at a time. The trick is that at no point are you to use any word that contains the letter S. Try it. Spoiler alert: it's impossible. It is a game that is set up to instigate failure. The best part is that the smiles and laughter come only when someone has failed. It generates a good group chuckle and reminds us that failure is not the end of the world.

8. Keep the big picture in perspective.

I'm a big-picture thinker, which means I don't get lost in the details. Not always helpful when attention is needed, but when it comes to being resilient, I believe it serves me well. Looking at situations from a big-picture perspective helps me to remember that I am more than any one situation. It allows me to see beyond the immediate, put present circumstances into context, and see the situation for what it is and not more. Look, shitty things have and will happen to all of us, and when it does, we need to have the tools to get through them and move beyond them. I'm talking about resilience, a topic well-covered by other books.

There are social protectors that contribute to resilience, and seeing our current circumstances for what they are and not more is one. The other option is to linger in the situation, but doing so gives it power and energy, and with that, it can grow. Have you ever heard of snowballing? It's irrationally attributing an isolated situation to something beyond it. Here are a few examples. You treat yourself to a pizza one night (and eat the whole thing), then chalk that up to an overall shitty diet, even though you've been eating well most other meals. From there, you proceed to cast yourself into this new character, who clearly has no self-control, and give yourself permission to continue your negative track. Classic self-sabotage. Unnecessary! Forgive yourself and move on. Also, what's so bad about eating a whole pizza? You get passed up for a promotion and decide that means you're undeserving and dumb. You allow yourself to settle into that new brand, and it keeps you from applying for other opportunities. You let it define you, and it takes control over your future. Wow—that's a lot of power to give to one unsuccessful job competition. Instead, ask for feedback, learn from it, and move on. Seek to develop your ability to compartmentalize. The shitty things that happen to you in your life don't have to define you. This is harder to do, the more severe the trauma, but the option is usually there.

Change your narrative. If you find yourself feeling like, or even being, the victim, focus on climbing out from that place by reminding yourself all that you have to be grateful for. When you look for it, you'll likely find that your fortunes are significantly greater than your misfortunes. And I'm not talking about money or material possessions. I'm talking about health, love, relationships, peace, opportunity, safety. Things that most of us are afforded simply by the country or environment in which we live.

Think about the experience of reading this book. Each chapter is unique. They all tell stories and provide takeaways, but no one chapter carries this book—they all are required. Also, as you read, remember to acknowledge that you don't know what lies ahead.

The completed chapters are done; you might know the chapter titles that lie ahead, but there is much to discover as you make your way through the book. When it comes to the past, the present, and the future, remember that where you are now is but a moment in time, the future is in the next word.

When shitty things happen to you, remember that you are experiencing a moment, perhaps even a full chapter's worth of words, but that the full story of who you are cannot be told through this one-chapter perspective. We are more than that.

9. Don't limit yourself.

This book has talked a lot about how our lack of confidence can limit the way we're seen and heard as leaders. But more importantly, doing so will limit your life experiences. Know that you can. Try. Believe in yourself. We only have one life; embrace it fully by getting out of your own way.

10. Flaunt.
Obviously.

CHAPTER 9

You, Out Loud

Everything that you want to be, you already are, and you are simply on the path of discovering it.
—Alicia Keys

Let me introduce you ... to you. You are a good person, who is doing their best in this world. You're living with some insecurity but deep down you know you are a good person. I'm sure you'll enjoy spending time getting to know yourself during this chapter. The unfiltered version. The authentic you. The only you.

They say the only constants in this world are death and taxes but that's not true. Another constant is that you are who you are. Yes, you will evolve and grow but at the core, you are who you are. With so much, never-ending change and uncertainty, let this constant give you stability.

Have you ever found yourself anxious, feeling unnerved, shaky on your feet?

Do you know what is at the center of this new mindfulness practice?

Why is it that yoga places great focus on breathing?

There's a common denominator here and that is being grounded, or what I call coming back into yourself. It's a wonderful thing to know that you can stabilize yourself and count on yourself—always—and when you do so, you will be **confident to the core**.

When I was young, we used to play hide-and-go-seek outside. The boundaries for the game took in several blocks. "Home base" was usually someone's front steps. There was a thrill to hiding and trying to get to home base before you got discovered. For some that thrill was exciting, for others anxiety-provoking, and for yet others it was both. Regardless, we all breathed a little easier when we reached home base. Those front steps represented safety from being caught. Sharing in the feeling of safety, it was the place where we all gathered at the end and laughed at the game.

It got me thinking, what is home base now for us? Where do we feel safe together? Where can I go? What can I do to create that same feeling of ease and comfort? The great news is that home base can reside within you. You can carry home base around with you. As adults, it is within our reach at all times. If today that feels out of reach, try working on some centering activities like breathwork, meditation, or yoga. The other thing you need is belief and confidence in yourself. Being able to trust that you are OK, that you can create safety for yourself, is paramount to being confident to the core. Your level of self-assuredness, together with a developed ability to ground yourself provides the foundation you need to build those front steps, that home base, within you.

When people ask how they can "show up" more confidently, I don't focus on hand gestures or fake smiles; instead I coach them through an inside-out process—drawing out the authentic you. Faking it doesn't cut it. People can tell. And perhaps even worse, when you fake it, you further reinforce to yourself that the real version of you isn't enough.

It is. I promise.

We've got some words to define here—**fake** and **authentic**—opposite ends of the spectrum.

We hear or see the word authentic so much. In books, social media, development programs, leadership talks. It's a terrible word. It's jargon, it's superfluous, and it's misleading. Telling someone to be the authentic version of themselves is like saying have a nose. Imagine. Hey Bren, make sure to be the authentic version of yourself in that meeting. Hey Bren, make sure to bring your nose to that meeting. Duh! Um, how can I be anything but authentic? Have you ever tried? Tried being someone other than yourself? OK, you're probably saying yes, Bren, I have. I've gone into situations and faked it, tried assuming the personality of someone I know who is super-outgoing and I was definitely not authentic. Wait—you started your rebuttal with "I," so it was you who went into the situation? And then you assumed someone else's personality? What if I said that was still you, authentically you, adapting your personality for the environment and crowd? Semantics, I know, but I believe it's very, very important to distinguish between fundamentally changing who you are at your core and acting a part. In fact, I'm going to argue that it's impossible to not be you—it's impossible to not be authentic.

Sometimes we put on another character by dressing differently, modifying our voice, or behaving in a way that is different from our usual ways, but these are superficial adjustments to our external selves. At our core, we are who we are. You can call these adjustments "being fake" or "acting," both of which carry negative connotations, but what they really are is the result of self-monitoring that landed in a decision that adapting would serve you well; and sometimes it does. For example, I am a very casual person, I speak in conversational language, and I often drop formalities, but when I was emceeing the Heart and Stroke Foundation's Research Awards and introducing medical professionals who were being recognized for their contributions to the field I didn't open with casual, humorous tactics. Instead I was on-script, respectful and polished. Was I acting? Fake? No, I was showing the room a more appropriate version of myself and it was absolutely still me.

There are also times when you've determined an adaptation would serve you well, and it doesn't. We've all been there. Delivering a message we didn't believe in or expressing an emotion that we weren't feeling. We've all been there, and it sucks. It feels fake and disingenuous. We know when we're faking it and, most often, others do too. You've been on the receiving end of this as well, when a manager has told you that you have to do something, yet you can tell that even they don't believe what they're saying. Gross.

Generally, though, being able to tack and adjust to the situation and our audience is a wonderful skill. The main point I want you to get here is that doing so does not make you inauthentic.

I get the sense you need more convincing. OK. I know a lot of people who are professional actors (no Ryan Goslings or anything but...) and they are some of the most grounded people I know. Does playing a role make them fakers? Does showing up as someone other than themselves make them inauthentic people? Frig, I hope not, I like these people! No, absolutely not. Here's the proof. Have you ever heard of a screen writer creating a role for a specific actor? Are you aware that casting professionals are hiring for more than just a "look?" The reason the "who" behind the role is so critical is that the writers know the actor will bring their unique self to the role. That's why there are auditions, not just a headshot. Beneath the hair and make-up, under the costumes and behind the lines is an actor who fills out the role with their authentic self—what other option do they have?

Here's the mind-blowing truth: there is only one version of you.

We have to believe that or else we're in for a lot of work. Think about it, having to grow, manage, and fine-tune multiple versions of you? If you're a perfectionist, I feel this would leave you very little time for much of anything else! So instead, let's focus on the one version of you (and of course, let's work on showing self-compassion by pulling away from perfectionism).

I'm sure many of you have used filters or Photoshopped your pictures. These are modifications to your image but at our core we are who we are, nothing changes. Instagram doesn't have the power to change you, it's no more powerful than putting on a mask or costume at Halloween—underneath it all, it's still you. There are filters to make us look better, smoother skin, more tanned, nicer lashes and they are fun but there is danger in overusing filters. This is a very real thing. I've heard from younger women that they use them so often that they don't like the way they look without them.

Look, I have a real agenda here. Ultimately, I'm wanting you to flaunt it and in a truly proud way. To do so, you must love yourself and then find the courage to show yourself to others. This all starts with knowing and accepting who you are. Over-filtering can make you fall in love with a modified version of yourself and when the filters aren't available, your confidence will fail you. That's why convincing you that the unfiltered version of you, the only *you* you have, is absolutely wonderful.

We've seen an uptake in the unfiltered movement on social media. I opened this chapter with an icon from this movement, Alicia Keys. She hasn't been seen wearing make-up for years and even when she was a judge on *The Voice*, she showed up *au naturel*. Such a powerful message to all of us. We are beautiful and deserving humans just as we are. Perfectly Imperfect. Why do we even wear make-up or do our hair and wear heels? I'd say it's because society tells us that being beautiful and deserving needs to have a certain look, act a certain way, and use particular words, so we apply filters and try hard to get there. I'm the first to say I feel more beautiful when I have mascara and some red lipstick on, but I know it's important for you and I to remember that we feel that way based on a societal norm or trend that is acting as our measuring stick for beauty. It's a comparative response. Go ahead and do what makes you feel good and confident, wear make-up if you want, dye your hair (I'm not naturally growing blonde hair these days), but please remember that who you are underneath it all, is you—naturally wonderful, you.

If I've done my job well, you now understand there is only one you—the "authentic" one—and you're about to propose to yourself and enter into a lifelong, unconditional loving relationship with yourself. Now, let's look at how to express it.

While I'm all about debunking societal norms and staying true to what feels right to you, I do know that we'd be better served considering our self-expression as it relates to environments and audiences. I'll use an extreme example to make my point. There is very little that makes me happier than wearing sweatpants and a hoodie (sans bra). In fact, I'm wearing that right now. But I do understand that there is a time and place for that special outfit, and it isn't in my corporate clients' boardrooms. Am I meant to deviate from my true identity and become something I'm not? Heck no.

First, if my "true identity" is wrapped up in my sweatpants, I have bigger problems. See, this is why our confidence has to be rooted in something deeper than our clothes or make-up or filters. I was a vice-president of a consulting company, and I was once sent home because I was wearing green nail polish. Absurd, yes. But I didn't own the company, I didn't make the rules. I could take offence and argue, but I'd lose because at the end of the day, the firm leaders called the shots. So I went home and treated myself to a manicure. I know some people who have been asked to remove their nose ring before coming to work, and while that doesn't feel good, the powers-that-be are allowed to ask that of you. It's not giving in, it's adapting your look in trade for corporate requirements. And frankly, it's no different from being asked to wear a uniform when you work at McDonald's. Navigating the balance that must be struck between expression of your true self and what is deemed appropriate by company or societal norms is tricky and personal (and a good topic to talk through with a mentor!). I encourage you to discover your balance.

We can learn a lot by picking up on cues from others whom we respect and seem to be doing it well. Looking back, we've seen some interesting trends in how women were showing up as leaders in the corporate world. In the late '80s and early '90s, women were still very much cast as subordinate players who helped their male bosses to succeed. Women who reached the top at that time had adopted the strategy that looking like men would make it easier for them to be seen as leaders, and it worked. Looking at pictures of women leader from that time, we see women with short hair, pant suits and shoulder pads—you know, to make them look bigger. In every way, they looked more like men. I can't blame them, competition was fierce. Not only did they have to work hard to be seen as a potential leader, they also had to work hard at beating out their fellow women. This became known as the Queen Bee Syndrome.

Recent articles suggest that the Queen Bee Syndrome is gone and that more women today are advocating for other women, making their climb to the top easier. Perhaps now the expression should be "Climb the ladder and throw down the rope."

Before we get too celebratory though, let's balance that research with some of qualitative experiences I've had. Whenever I talk about the Queen Bee Syndrome and how it's all but vanished, I see eye rolls and hear sarcastic chuckles. I worked with hundreds of women at a major US technology company and they were quite clear in telling me that at their company, women leaders are bitchy and cutthroat. With such contradictory evidence, the question is, are the leadership behaviours we are seeing from women today truly unsupportive of other women or are they simply not what we expect to see from women leaders?

Look, I know both men and women leaders can be highly competitive, blunt and even downright seemingly insensitive, but perhaps this doesn't mean they are not also championing other women at senior tables or otherwise actively removing barriers to advancement. Our mental models expect women leaders be empathetic, compassionate, and collaborative in their approach to decision-making. All of this is to say that one's leadership style may not be linked to one's efforts at increasing gender equality.

I am optimistic that, like the evolution in dressing for corporate leadership roles, how we show up as leaders will continue to evolve so that we no longer feel other women are a threat to our success. I see it often, women throwing down the rope. I've witnessed senior women in aerospace, mining, transportation, finance, and other sectors establish and run organized groups aimed at supporting the development and advancement of other women in their industries. I've presented at conferences alongside very established women who were speaking *for free* to large groups of aspiring women, all in an effort to inspire and encourage them. I know there are some women leaders who are tough to work for, just as there are men, but let's do ourselves a big favour and drop this stereotype—it's either outdated or, at the very worst, it's becoming a self-fulfilling prophecy. After all, there is no male equivalent to the Queen Bee Syndrome.

They are all playing the political game and women leaders need to spend their capital wisely, just as men do. If you don't see this going on in your company, make sure you're doing it—be the change you wish to see.

Flaunting is about feeling and projecting confidence. Earlier chapters helped you strengthen your inner confidence; now it's time to look at how to show your confidence, outwardly, to the world. And it matters. Imagine if I walked into a room, took a seat, pulled out a notebook, pen, and three devices, sat them all beside my tea and protein bar. When called upon in the meeting, I meekly said, "I think we should hire two new people for the project." How do you think it would be received?

First of all, everyone else in the room would have to try to find me behind all of the shit I brought to the meeting. Seriously, a laptop and glass of water should get you through a one-hour meeting. Do you want to be seen as the notetaker or the ideas person? Pay attention to the role you cast yourself in.

Secondly, no matter how good your ideas are, if you talk about them in an underwhelming, diminishing way, no one will take you seriously, and, in fact, they might not hear you at all.

Showing up strong is all about saying what you're great at in a confident way! This means standing tall, owning your space, using your full voice, and making eye contact.

The number one most common complaint I hear from women is that they get interrupted by others in meetings. Before I tell you how to decrease the number of times people interrupt you, I must say that I consider interruptions to be a good thing. Most often, they indicate engagement, showing that people are listening and interested in your topic or idea. Maybe they have a pivotal question, or a point that could add value to the conversation. Yes, they could have waited their turn, and yes, we've been told that interrupting is not polite, but I'd rather have someone cut me off because they are so into my talk than have them looking at their phones. That said, should you encounter a repeat offender, a habitual interrupter, you certainly should address it. Use the STAR model from the "Sticky Situations" chapter to guide you through this tough conversation.

OK, now onto how to minimize interruptions. You've heard the expression "hold the room"? This means getting the attention of those in the room and keeping it—not always easy in a world full of distractions and competing priorities. Let's start with this fact: I am very seldomly interrupted. Why? What am I doing differently that signals to others not to interrupt me? It's not magic, it's not charisma, it's not extroversion, it's not an outgoing personality—none of these things are required. You can project confidence exactly as you are today. It's you, at your best. It's you unfiltered. And it's you out loud.

You *got* this! Here are seven ways to project confidence.

1. Stand tall. Yes, stand. Your presence is automatically strengthened when you stand. There are a lot of reasons for this. One, you're assuming the leader's role when you stand—it's like you have the talking stick. Two, you are easier to see and hear when you stand. Three, you are better able to read the room, and pivot as needed, when you have a clear view of your audience. And four, standing allows you to have a good speaking stance, one that opens your body language, and feeds you full breaths to fuel your voice. Stand up now—let's practice.

So now you're standing, nice work. Oh wait—stand up just a touch taller. There you go. We tend to make ourselves small, shrink our height (even if you're not tall, but especially if you are), and roll in our shoulders. It's like we're hiding our boobs. It's OK, we have them, and they get to sit where they belong, so roll your shoulders back, chest up. No need to stand stiff and at attention, but do stand strong, with pride.

What are you supposed to do with your arms and legs and hips? I know, it feels awkward at first. Start with your feet. Get grounded. Stand with your feet shoulder-width apart with fifty percent of your weight on each leg. Resist the urge to relax into one hip. Many women naturally stand with one hip popped out. For some this is because they carried a child around on that hip for years, and for others it's a way to reduce our height, but it can give a sexy vibe. For real. We don't have to like it, but that is how an audience may perceive us when we deliver our message with a hip out. And that's a risk I want to minimize, I don't want or need to look sexy when I'm speaking. I don't want my audience distracted by my body, I want them focused on my words. So, feet apart, standing strong from the ground up, allow your body to feel anchored, solid, as you stand there. You are so powerful in this stance. Unfaltering.

Now, turn your attention to your arms and hands. We tend to close them either by crossing our arms, putting them in our pockets, or clasping them in front of us. All of this is considered closed body language. Think about it! Crossed arms is literally putting an X between you and your audience. Hands in your pocket, what are you hiding in there? I don't trust you. And clasping and/or rubbing your hands/fingers together makes you look nervous, not confident. It's self-soothing behaviour and it's one step away from giving yourself a little hug—not a great look for a leader.

So, what are you supposed to do with your hands? Use them to help you tell your story. Gesture! I find it so funny how unnatural people feel when I call attention to their arms and ask them to gesture, especially considering that we do so very naturally in everyday conversation. It's true! Imagine this, you're at a café having a coffee or glass of wine with a friend. You've just come back from a trip, and you're telling your friend all about the best bits. My guess is that you use your arms quite naturally; they become an extension of your storytelling. I don't want you to choreograph your moves; I simply ask that you free your arms to do what they naturally want to do in helping you express yourself.

Standing this way and using your arms will take practice; it takes conditioning. Get yourself in shape for the opportunity. Work on being able to stand for 30 minutes in a strong stance. I do this by taking every phone call standing. Give it a try!

Go ahead and give yourself permission to take up the space that your body rightfully deserves. There's no need to minimize your greatness; showing up strong requires us to feel strong in every way, from the feet up.

2. Start with a bang. Remember to get to your point quickly and use confident language. You learned how to write a message in "Sticky Situations," and we cleared away weak language in "Bad Words," replacing them instead with the confident language found in "Good Words."

3. Look them in the eye. Make eye contact with your audience to show them your conviction. I can assure you that when you're at home telling someone to pick up their socks, you're not staring into the distance; you're looking them straight in the eye to ensure the message has been received. It shows your audience that you believe what you're saying, and you want them to believe it as well. It also keeps your audience accountable. It's very difficult for someone to look away, pick up their phone, and start texting someone when you're looking at them.

Again, I want you to use conversational eye contact just as you'd use back at the café with your friend; nothing forced. And if you want to gauge how much eye contact is right, watch your audience and give them what they give you; they're telling us what they are comfortable with. As their comfort increases, so will their eye contact.

4. Use your full voice. Sound like you want to be taken seriously. Our voices are very personal; it's how you've sounded your whole life. Now I'm asking you to audit your voice and determine if any changes are needed so that you can project all of your confidence. What does confidence sound like? To start with, it requires your voice to be heard. You'd be surprised how many people tell me that when they are in meetings, it's like they're not being heard. In many cases, it is very likely that they actually aren't being heard because they are speaking so quietly! If you aren't sure whether you're speaking loudly enough, ask someone for feedback. Another vocal tool to activate is your "I'm speaking" tone. It's the tone that says you want to be heard. It's not a cute, girly voice. It's not sweet or endearing. It's strong and confident. It takes a good amount of breath to fuel that kind of voice. Try it now. Take a big breath in, and say a sentence, any sentence, out loud in your strongest voice. It might feel "too much" or "too powerful," but it's you at your most confident self so catch up to it, practice it and use it often.

There are a few vocal habits that are worth mentioning. *Upspeak* is when your voice rises at the end of a sentence, as if it's a question. The issue is that you sound like you're questioning your own ideas, which is not terribly convincing. The other habit is *vocal fry*, that thing people do when they're trying to sound cool by making their voice nasally, raspy, and throaty. It sounds casual and gives a tone of I-don't-give-a-fuck. Neither of these vocal habits help to project confidence in any way. If you want to increase your awareness of your vocal habits, I recommend using your phone's voice recorder and playing your voice back to yourself. Painful but necessary.

In virtual meetings and phone calls, you are two-dimensional, which means your voice carries even greater importance. It's all you have to project confidence.

5. Take your time. We'll wait. The pace at which you speak has a huge impact on projecting confidence. Some of you might be fast talkers. You know who you are. There are many reasons why people speak too quickly; one is that they truly believe that it's more efficient—I mean, you *can* squeeze more words into less time. But if your audience is having a hard time following you, they will disengage. And they will have a hard time keeping up because the rate at which you are speaking may be appropriate for you—you've thought about what you're going to say, maybe even practiced it—but your audience is hearing it for the first time. You're more familiar with your content than your audience, and since them hearing you, following you, and understanding you is what matters most, you have to deliver your talk at the pace that's best for them. Another reason some folks speak quickly is to get it over with. You're nervous; you hate speaking in front of a crowd; and when you talk too quickly, it shows. Again, not a good strategy for projecting confidence.

Since we're interested in making sure our audience stays engaged, give them time to digest what you're saying by using pauses throughout your talk. Pausing when it suits us is why people enjoy reading.

As you're reading this now, you're pausing when you need to digest what you've just read. You can even go back and reread a sentence if you want. Reading gives the audience the luxury of setting their own pace, but with verbal communication the speaker sets the pace. As you look at this page, you'll see that there are periods at the end of each sentence and that the text is broken up into separate paragraphs. Sometimes there even headings within chapters highlighting specific content. When you speak, let the audience hear this punctuation; they need time to reflect on the brilliant ideas you're sharing.

Also this: I've never told anyone to speak more quickly.

6. Be fun to watch! Consider this: How do you look and sound when you read to a child? It's like we all turn into Disney characters or stage actors. In a word, I'd say my performance is dynamic. It's fueled with energy; we don't hold anything back. We use a range in our voices to take on the various characters, we act out the motions, and we are entirely audience focused. We stop worrying about how we look; all our focus is on putting on a great show for the kid. Truth is, as an audience member at two o'clock in a Tuesday afternoon meeting I have the attention span of a two-year-old. Please give the same energy to all of your audiences.

7. Own your power. The world is ready for the full version of you! Sometimes I hear that these techniques feel "*too* strong." This presents a mental challenge to stepping fully into your power. To know, without a doubt, that you deserve to be heard and respected can fly in the face of how we usually, comfortably show up, which places great emphasis on being liked. Liked vs. respected. This is a fun conversation I often have with my coaching clients. What is more important to you as a leader? Some truthfully admit that being liked is a driving factor in their presence, and honestly, I can usually guess that about them. How? Well, the need to be liked can undermine our delivery. It often shows up as over-smiling, minimizing body language, or a speaking with a cute voice. Perhaps you too would prefer to be liked rather than respected. I urge you to consider how that deflates the power of your message, and the signal it gives to the audience about how you want to be perceived. Clearly, we'd like to be both liked *and* respected but my priority in just about all of my relationships is to be respected. I want my friends to respect me, my colleagues, my partner, and my family. We naturally have a pretty good likability factor, so instead I'd recommend working on developing respect.

Some of these tips might at first feel strange when you implement them because it's not what you're used to. Standing with open arms, speaking with greater volume or more slowly can seem unnatural, and that's OK. I want you to remember that, when you're speaking, your audience are the most important people in the room, not you. Everything you say and how you say it is for the audience; after all, they are the only reason why you're talking at all! So, embrace the discomfort until it becomes comfortable. It's like a new pair of shoes; you like how they look, but they feel terrible on your feet at first. A committed fashionista will break those puppies in until they are comfortable. The same is true with these techniques, and the payoff is equally rewarding.

Whoever you are right now, just as you are, is more than enough. You are enough.

It's time to stop shrinking, whispering, disappearing. Stand tall, speak up, be seen. The world needs more of you!

CHAPTER 10

Flaunt Your Face Off

Hey you! What's your hidden talent?

FUN! OK, next question, why is it *hidden*?

You have a talent, many talents in fact, that most people don't know you have, even some people who are very close to you. But why the big secret? If people don't know what you have to offer, how can they appreciate it, draw on it, learn from it, benefit from it? Imagine if I was super-amazing at public speaking but no one in my company knew it. Poor Steve in Operations keeps getting dragged on stage to present, and he hates it and is terrible at it. Meanwhile, I'm down the hall, sitting on my spectacular speaking skills. This would be a disservice to everyone—Steve, the company, the audience, and—here's the big part—me! Opportunities to work in your passion areas are much more likely to come your way when you share your talents. It's our job to make sure others know our value.

If you want to get promoted, you'd better be able to promote yourself. And you have to mean it. Have you ever had someone sell you something that you know they would never buy themselves? Yeah, it doesn't work. It's your job to get noticed. Generally speaking, people don't wake up thinking about how they can make your life better, get you a promotion, or help you achieve your goals. That's why you have to know what you want, know that you're worth it, and then flaunt to bring attention to why you deserve it.

Why else should you flaunt? Flaunting can do some amazing things for you. Here are four ways flaunting can help you:

1. You will appear more confident in conversations. By speaking about your wins, you'll be radiating confidence. People pay attention to what you talk about. Interactions are opportunities to tell people how to perceive you (more on this below).
2. You will adopt a more positive mindset and improve your well-being. Flaunting feeds your mind with all the good stuff. By focusing on what you're doing well instead of your faults, your stress and anxiety will lessen, and your attitude will position you for even more wins!
3. Your love for yourself will grow. When you sell yourself to others, you're also selling yourself to you. Flaunting reminds you of all the wonderful value that you offer to the world.
4. Others will become more aware of your value, and new opportunities will emerge. The fact is, to convince others that you are ready for a promotion or new challenges, you must be able to promote yourself. Flaunting unlocks the mystery for others about how they can get the best from you.

Making sure people know about your talents, wins, and accomplishments is known as *self-promotion*, and if you haven't figured it out yet, I want you to become a self-promoter. You already bought (or borrowed) a book called *Flaunt*, so something tells me you're open to the idea. Now that you're in the final chapter, you're ready. Ready to learn the "how-to" of flaunting. But before we get there, we have to talk about why we recoil and why our skin crawls at the very thought of flaunting.

The truth is, that for many of you, flaunting is very uncomfortable (that's why I wrote this book). Close your eyes for a minute and think about the word flaunt. What image comes to your mind? People have told me it conjures up images of people being loud and boastful. Ugh, yuck, no thank you. This is precisely why it is outside of most people's comfort zones to actively promote their value. Flaunting seems contrary to the idea of being humble and polite, which we have been taught since we were young. However, repressing our awareness of our greatness (and yes, you have greatness) only deepens the insecurities that were brought on through socialization, upbringing, and gender roles, which are then further reinforced through pop culture. So, how do we strike that balance of feeling and projecting confidence while not coming across as arrogant? The answer is humility.

When I was about 14, my father told me that I would always struggle with humility. Truth be told, I had absolutely no idea what he was talking about. I didn't even know what the word meant. I did know that I was a confident girl, and I was curious to know what this struggle was going to be. It was many, many years later before I learned, and I learned it through observing others. Working with executives, I see it all. Real arrogance. Deep insecurity (humility overdone). All of it.

I once coached a director at an energy company who had recently returned from a big meeting in Texas with oil executives. The host of the meeting was a billionaire. The meeting attendees all piled into the large mahogany boardroom and took their seats. Almost as soon as they sat down, one of them spilled their coffee all over the table. The host (the billionaire) promptly got out of his seat, sourced some cleaner and paper towel, and began cleaning up the mess. Upon seeing this, one of the attendees said something like, "Man, don't you have people for that?" The host replied, "When I'm too good to clean up spilled coffee, I'm done." My client was wowed. It changed him as a man to witness that interaction. As we debriefed it, we both concluded that it truly was an expression of humility. No leader is perfect; spills happen.

This story is consistent with my experience of working with senior leaders. In fact, my observation is that the higher up the ladder you go, the humbler the leader. My theory for this is that as they advance, they come to realize how little they know and how much they rely on others' knowledge and support for their success.

Anchoring yourself in humility is the key to staving off arrogance.

I'm not perfect, neither are you. We're all faking it and just doing our best. But that doesn't mean I don't have talents. It doesn't take away from my accomplishments. It doesn't mean I can't feel proud of myself. And it doesn't mean I can't speak well of myself, to myself and others. We are so quick to own our flaws and mistakes, but so slow to celebrate our good bits and wins. When is the last time you looked in the mirror and *only* said one nice thing about yourself and then walked away? So many of us do the opposite: we look in the mirror, see a flabby tummy, groan at ourselves, and then walk away. I want you to try it: the next time you're near a mirror, I want you to spot something wonderful—maybe it's your great eyes, your hair, or your strong arms—give yourself a smile, and then walk away. Don't negate it by lingering around and noting something negative; we can all do that. It's just healthier not to.

The difference between confidence and arrogance is the presence of humility, or the lack thereof.

This book aims to remove shame from flaunting and redefine it as radiating confidence from the inside out. It's about how you view and express yourself. How you share yourself with the world.

By minimizing your insecurities and fears and boosting your courage and confidence, you can enhance your life experiences, and who doesn't want that?

This isn't about showing off; it's about radiating what's true. Feeling proud and showing it is healthy self-promotion.

Flaunt without apology. Remember the chapter "Bad Words"? Disclaimers take the power out of your flaunt, so remember to avoid disclaimers like:

It was no big deal.

I don't mean to brag, but…

I was just lucky.

Sorry to toot my own horn, but…

Correct skeptics.

There may be people who are uncomfortable with seeing you flaunt, but remember that you're part of the start of a movement—one where we're redefining flaunting as being something that's positive. Most likely, people will be inspired themselves to flaunt when seeing you flaunt. The opposite of confidence is not humility; the opposite of arrogance is humility. When people are arrogant, they lack humility. Humility is the ability to recognize that you are not always right and that you don't have all of the answers. Being humble does not mean having a poor opinion of yourself but recognizing that others are equally valuable. With that definition, you can see that you can be confident and humble, but you cannot be arrogant and humble. When someone labels your flaunt as bragging or arrogance, set them straight. Tell them that you're feeling proud of a win or confidence in a talent, and you're sharing it with others. It's not a bad thing, but, in fact, a wonderful thing. It's generating positivity, it's giving others permission to do the same. Let me ask you this: would you rather hear someone complain about traffic or tell you about a big win they had at work today? Don't dim your light so others can shine. Or, as Marianne Williamson says in *A Return to Love: Reflections on the Principles of "A Course in Miracles,"* "There is nothing enlightened about shrinking so that other people won't feel insecure around you.... And as we let our own light shine, we unconsciously give other people permission to do the same."

Because flaunting is tough for most of us, and because I'm hoping to start a massive movement here, I call on you to **cheer on fellow flaunters!** When you hear someone say something nice about themselves, or a success they've had, celebrate it. Congratulate them! High-fives all around! By doing so, you'll encourage them and others to feel safe to express themselves in this way and build their confidence—one flaunt at a time.

You may be wondering what constitutes a flaunt. Do I have to get a promotion or run a marathon to flaunt? Absolutely not! In fact, you're encountering flaunt-worthy wins several times a day. The shitty part is that, until now, they've gone unnoticed. Unnoticed by others, because we don't share them, and unnoticed by you, thereby missing out on many opportunities every day to build your confidence. It's important to notice the wins along the way. Others may overlook the work it took you to achieve your success, but it's important that you do not. Acknowledging all of the hard work and wins along the way will contribute to positive self-confidence. I want you to unapologetically celebrate every step you took towards success.

Here's the thing: flaunting takes confidence, celebrates confidence, and generates more confidence.

So, how do you begin to spot your flaunt-worthy talents? To give you an idea, here are a few of my flaunts from today ... so far ... it's 1:13 p.m.

I got up, ready, and out the door for an 8 a.m. flight ... and looked fabulous.

I wrote 3,800 words in this book today (and still going).

I'm having dinner with a friend from my MBA program, whom I've done a good job keeping in touch with over the 13 years since we graduated.

I reached out to my partner's sister to wish her a good trip.

I made sure my dog was picked up and cared for in a timely manner.

I checked on friends on the east coast, following a recent hurricane.

I connected with my guy and reminded him how special he is to me.

I practiced self-care (French onion soup and a glass of red wine for lunch!).

Did I mention it's only 1:13? I'm unstoppable.

Your turn. Stop right now and make a list of all that you've accomplished already today. I'm confident that you'll come up with at least five. Do it now ... and then do it every day.

Imagine you're in an interview and someone asks you, "What's so good about you?" Do you have an answer ready? If not, spend some time this week taking inventory of your strengths, skills, and accomplishments and prepare your answer!

OK, let's practice. Here are a few springboards I offer that will necessarily launch you into a fabulous flaunt:

"I'm absolutely amazing at..."

"A win I had today was..."

"I'm proud of myself for…"

"I love myself today because…"

The best flaunts are those that *acknowledge **your** successes*, not those of others. It must be something you did. I taught a course to a group of women in mining and had them stand up and finish the statement "Something I'm proud of is…" It was interesting to hear many of them mention something their children did. One said, "My daughter had two good naps today." Ummmmm, that wasn't your accomplishment; she was the one who slept. Instead, say, "A win I had today was that I cared for my daughter in a way that allowed her to get the sleep she needed." See the difference?

How to flaunt is an inside-out process—feel it, flaunt it. I don't want superficial flaunts. I want heartfelt flaunts, the kind that make you blush at first but then make you stand a little taller, smile a little bigger, and give you that warm feeling of pride that washes over you. There's nothing like it.

People ask us how things are going, personally or professionally, and almost always our response is about what's not working. A mistake or weakness, something that's gone wrong. It's like a confessional! But their question wasn't, "How have you fucked up lately?" When people ask me how things are going, I use it as an opportunity to flaunt, almost always. Why not? It's better for the world, and it's better for me. Here's some flaunting in action. People often ask, "What do you do?" and you likely respond with your job title, which is not an appropriate answer to that question. Instead, think: What *do* you do? Here's my answer: "I equip and encourage others to radiate confidence." Your turn! What do *you* do? Tip: Begin your response with an action verb.

I'm not ignorant of my weaknesses; I simply choose not to give them a ton of air time, with others or myself. We can learn from our mistakes while acknowledging our wins. The way I see it, we are not punching bags; we can't take constant blows. If we're going to beat ourselves up over our losses, we'd better be spending at least as much time celebrating our wins. We are so quick to own our failures and weaknesses, even when others were involved. But, when given the same degree of ownership and responsibility for our wins, we become fearful. Don't be afraid of the power of ownership. Don't shy away from winning. I talk about my mistakes and weaknesses with my sister and other close friends when I need to, but I know everyone, including me, benefits from flaunts. Wins breed more wins—for me and others. It's that simple.

Embrace the whole process—from setting the goal to going the distance to crossing the finish line. It may feel unnatural at first to give yourself credit for everything you do, but do yourself a huge favour, and *get used to it*!

You might say that flaunting doesn't come naturally to you. Perhaps you're an introvert and sharing your thoughts out loud isn't you. To that, I would respond that being an introvert means you get your energy from being alone, and for that reason, you tend to shy away from special attention. Flaunting may seem unnatural to introverts, but the benefits are just as real to you as they are to extroverts. Don't use your introversion as an excuse. Having confidence, acknowledging your wins, and sharing them with others is good for everyone.

But when is the right time to flaunt? Don't wait for an invitation to self-promote. Rarely do people say, "Tell me about a win you had this week." Flaunting isn't reserved for special occasions, like performance reviews. By the way, how do you think your boss gathers information for your performance review? Much of it is based on what they hear (not see), so make sure you are sharing your wins with them. A casual run-in with a senior leader, a dinner table with eager ears, and a hangout with friends can all be great times to flaunt! People are too busy to notice all of your wins. That's why it's your job to keep them informed.

I self-promote in the areas that are aligned with my brand. I rarely promote my excellent swimming skills because that doesn't help me now; it's not relevant. I do self-promote my writing skills; *aren't I great?*

There's a lot of talk these days about our personal brand: *"What's your brand?"* Seems lofty, I mean, most of us are going through life doing what we do, doing our best most days. Having a clearly defined brand and managing it seems like a lot of work, perhaps a job for a marketing expert, but not for us. If this is what you think, you're not wrong. It is a lot of work. However, I'm going to show you why it's worth the effort. There is much to be gained by dialing into your brand, being clear on how you want to be seen and what you want to be known for, and as importantly, how you don't.

Let's begin by defining what a brand *is*. A brand is a group of assigned attributes for a product, service, or person. Basically, it's a shortcut for what we think about something or someone based on our perceptions of it. A brand can be established through one of two ways. The first way is through your own experience of a product, service, or person, or through the experiences of someone you hold in high regard. Let's call these the "real deal" and the "referral." If it is your own experience, the real deal, then it requires multiple interactions with the product, service, or person before it becomes a brand in your mind. Rarely do we interact with something or someone and immediately assign it strong brand qualities, and if we do, I'd say we might be too quick to judge. Rather, it takes time. I've never used a product only once and then became a lifelong loyal customer. That kind of brand loyalty takes time. If a brand was solidified through referral, what has happened is that someone whose opinion you trust and value has assigned their credibility to the brand. We often see this happening among family members or close friends. These days, social media influencers are getting rich on this premise alone. They're using their fame to promote a product or service, and we're buying because we think they are cool/smart/fun, whatever the reason.

The main point I want to make here is that your brand is simply others' perceptions of you, and you have full control over how you show up in the world. What you *don't* have control over is other people's disposition or attitude when receiving you. This requires us to be audience-centered—basically, read the room. I might want my brand to include positivity (which it does), but that doesn't mean I should constantly present myself as over-the-top positive. The first obvious reason being that I'm not always feeling uber-positive, and faking it doesn't work—in fact, that would have an adverse effect on my brand. The second reason is that I must be mindful, empathetic, to the person or people I'm engaging with. If a friend has just lost her job, it's likely not the best time for me to push her to see the good in the world. I will eventually, since gratitude goes a long way, but in the short term, what my friend needs is empathy, listening. She needs me to meet her where she's at, not force my brand on her. But since none of us have control over the receiving side of perception, let's call it net neutral. And with that, we can attest that we do, in fact, have full control over our brand.

Back to perceptions. If a brand is based on others' perceptions, it's important to consider how they are created, and the answer is in how you behave and communicate.

It's time! Let's examine your brand. Yes, your brand! You do know that you already have one, right? Oh boy, this can be scary to think about. Yes, you already have one. It may not be exactly the brand you want, but you do have one. You see, you've been behaving and communicating before reading this; therefore, you've planted your brand attributes in the minds of others, and it has been established. For a simple brand audit, I'd like you to complete this activity. Imagine I called ten people in your life—people who work with you, your boss, a friend—and I asked them to tell me three words they would use to describe you. What would they say? Now, as you do this, don't be particularly mean or particularly kind to yourself—be as honest as possible. Want to make this real? Remove your assumptions about your brand and actually ask these people that question. Come on, do it! It takes courage, but it's a reality check and will provide you with insight about what your brand truly is today. Most often, when I do this exercise with clients, their self-assessment of their brand is very close to what they hear back when asking others for this feedback, but sometimes it is not.

A few years ago, I was coaching a female client of a multinational corporation who was vying for the CEO role. She was already a member of the executive team, so it was safe to assume she was a strong candidate. I was hired to help her prepare for and navigate the promotion process. I began by asking her about her brand. She reported to be seen in a very similar way to my initial take on her—smart, kind, and capable. Because so much was at stake, I decided to go beyond our chat and reach out to others in the organization. I connected with people who reported to her, her colleagues on the executive team, and her boss, the current CEO. The results came in anonymously to me, and I was dumbfounded. It wasn't good. In two words? *Ice Queen.* Everyone described her as cold, impersonal, and uncaring. You don't have to be an expert to know that this brand wasn't going to cut it for her to become the leader of the company. Think about it: would you want someone like this as a boss? A colleague? Absolutely not. So, we got to work and did all we could to rebrand her as quickly as possible. We were unsuccessful, mainly because rebranding takes time, especially brands that require a significant shift in a short amount of time. I'm happy to report that she has since left that company and is now the CEO of another large company. That's what was needed for her to show up differently. She needed a clean slate, a fresh audience with whom she could behave and communicate differently, thereby generating a new leadership brand that was aligned with who she was and who the organization needed her to be as their leader.

When you ask others for their three words they would use to describe you, you may hear some words that leave you feeling proud and others that don't. That's OK! We're all a work in progress, and remember, you can rebrand yourself the same way you've branded yourself already: by intentionally behaving and communicating in a way that projects the brand words you'd like people to use to describe you. Here comes the next part of this activity: defining your *desired* brand.

To help guide your behaviour and communication, it's good to have a goal in mind. What three words would you like people to use to describe you? As you generate this list, challenge yourself to move beyond mediocre words like hardworking, organized, and knowledgeable. While these are great words, and I'd love for someone to say them about me, they are not strong, powerful, leadership words.

What words would you use to describe a leader? Think now of someone who you admire; it can be someone you know, perhaps a previous boss or a parent, or someone famous who projects the qualities you'd like to emulate. What are three words you'd use to describe them? I first thought up this exercise when working with

30 software engineers from Microsoft. When I asked them for their current brand words, they pretty much all said smart, hardworking, and detail-oriented. Cool. Great words, but there are two problems with those words. First, everyone in the room is the same as you, so how will you stand out? And second, none of them sounded like leaders. Look, you're all being paid to be smart, hardworking, and detail-oriented. That's what the paycheck is for every two weeks. But what else? What makes you so special? Seriously, what makes you so special? What is your differentiator? Stretch yourself when defining your desired brand. You are free to include words that don't describe you today but that you'd like to work towards. My current brand is confident (clearly), positive, and bold. And while I love these words and they do accurately describe me, I have a few tweaks to my brand that I'm working on. My desired brand is confident (can't lose that one), inspiring, and determined. Subtle changes, for sure, but a pivot, nonetheless. So, what can we do to become known as our desired brand?

Now that you've assessed your current brand and defined your desired brand, it's time to bridge the gap. Become very intentional in your actions and words, in your stillness and silence. Every interaction counts. The mic is always on, and people are constantly gathering data on you by paying attention to what you say, how you say it, what you do, and how you do it. Let's look at each of these, one at a time.

What you say.
Walk around complaining about where the stapler is, and that's what you become known for. Constantly shoot down others' ideas, and that's what you become known for. Bring only problems and not solutions; yup, it goes toward your brand. Straight-up professional

in meetings, but love to gossip at the watercooler? Be careful; every word, every interaction matters. Your brand can't waver based on location. It's too confusing. Imagine if Starbucks coffee only tasted yummy when consumed in the store but terrible when you're drinking it walking down the street. A brand needs to be consistent everywhere, all of the time.

How you say it.
Remember our chapters on language. Using strong words will help to cement the brand you desire because they are not hesitant, cautious, or weak. There are other ways we can weaken our brand through communication, which we covered in the chapter "You, Out Loud." Deliver your ideas with confidence, strength, certainty, and presence.

What we talk about and the words we use can significantly impact our brand. What you say and how you say it. If you heard me saying, "By working together, we'll be able to achieve our shared goals," what word would you use to describe me? Team player? Collaborative? Exactly. To make that perception a brand, I'd have to communicate like this consistently, and eventually those words would stick.

I invite you to begin paying attention to your outer talk track. A good way to do this is to revisit your previous emails. You did this when looking for language traps in our earlier chapter, but this time, do it to see *what* you're talking about and *how* you're talking about it. What topics do you talk about most? What is your tone? Are these things consistent with how you want to be seen? I've met a lot of people who overwhelmingly talk about the negative, and it's draining. You know what it's like. Watch yourself, listen to yourself. Put yourself in the position of your audience. Doing so will increase your self-awareness.

What you do.
Ever hear the expression, "Actions speak louder than words"? Here, we're talking about observable behaviour. You want to be known as approachable? Show it! Put yourself on the hot seat and invite people in. It's not enough to say, "My door is always open," if, in fact, your door is never open. As you can see, your actions and words must match. If you say you're a team player, but, in fact, you work alone and without collaboration, you'll fail at being known as a team player. Words matter, but they alone are not enough. People trust what they can see.

How you do it.
Check yourself. This is all about the attitude with which you interact with others. Let's continue with the aspiration of being seen as a team player. You can say that you want to work with others; you can invite others to the room; but how you work with them matters. Are you dominating the conversation or listening well? Are you distracted with other things or fully engaged? Are you discounting others' ideas or inviting suggestions? We're not always in the mindset needed to behave in a way that positively promotes our brand. We all have bad days, bad moments, stressors, and distractions. That's why I started with the caution to check yourself. Not always, but sometimes you can choose to not engage if you know you won't do your brand justice. At times when you can't, heighten your awareness of your mental state, give yourself a talking to, and remind yourself that how you interact in this moment is going to count towards your brand—for good or bad—and do what you can to mitigate any damage.

Getting comfortable with flaunting requires us to get over "rumble strips" that warn us to stay in our lane and follow outdated social norms. Sharing our successes with others (flaunting) is valuable to others. You have to feel it and flaunt it. Start by noticing your wins and feeling a sense of pride; it's good for our mental health. Shame and guilt are social emotions designed to make sure we follow social norms, but not flaunting is a social norm that we should be trying to break. I'm all about changing social norms and making it easier for others to feel pride and share wins with others. Noticing wins helps us to have more wins! Flaunting is a behaviour, and you can choose to do it. Make flaunting part of your daily wellness program.

Let's count nine ways to incorporate flaunting into your life:

1. Tune in to your inner soundtrack and feed your mind with positive self-talk.
2. Celebrate your wins—out loud!
3. Keep track of your accolades by creating a flaunt file.
4. Take charge of your personal brand—how do you want to be perceived?
5. Acknowledge your successes, and feel proud.
6. Say what you want and share your ideas in a confident way!
7. Tell yourself daily affirmations like "I am enough!"
8. Recognize the role others play in your life and celebrate them.
9. Practice self-care to rest and strengthen those flaunting muscles.

People are ready to express, accept, and value genuineness like never before. The world is ready for you.

Go flaunt your face off.

Acknowledgments

It is no exaggeration to say that you would not be reading this book without the guidance of my sister, Gillian Landry. She helped to manage the project, held me accountable to timelines, listened to my rough ideas, read, and reread every single word, gave hours every Saturday for "book meetings", and has consistently been my biggest champion. It's no surprise, really. My sister has played all of these roles for me in all aspects of my life. I'm so fortunate to have such a fabulous, talented, caring big sis.

This book was written over several years. Years that saw me experience significant change such as losing a parent, moving provinces, and starting my own business. I wish to express my appreciation to all of my friends and mentors who supported me throughout these times. Specifically, Maggie Patten for driving me and my yellow lab Daisy to our new home in Toronto, and never leaving our side since. And to Casey Lynn and Claudia Milicevic for your ongoing guidance, friendship, kindness, and perpetually open door.

As a first-time author, there is much to learn throughout the writing and publishing process. I am grateful to have landed in the conscientious, capable, and kind hands of my publisher David Stover at Rock's Mills Press. Thank you, David, for having the confidence in me and this writing, and for understanding the importance of this book's message.

Throughout the writing process, I recruited readers to provide feedback on my writing and their contributions improved the quality of this book. Thanks to all who participated in this process as readers. Special shout out to Eva Martinez and Alycia Putnam.

And finally, every client I've worked with who has offered me the chance to continue learning through their experiences. I was only able to write what I know by learning from you.

Works Cited

Catalyst. (2021). *Women on Corporate Boards (Quick Take)*. www.catalyst.org/research/women-on-corporate-boards/.

Catalyst. (2022). *Women in Management (Quick Take)*. www.catalyst.org/research/women-in-management/.

Clance, P. R., & Imes, S. A. (1978). The imposter phenomenon in high achieving women: Dynamics and therapeutic intervention. *Psychotherapy: Theory, Research & Practice, 15*(3), 241–247.

Nicholson, Nigel. (1998, July-August). How hardwired is human behavior? *Harvard Business Review.* www.hbr.org/1998/07/how-hardwired-is-human-behavior.

Fiorina, Carly. (2006). *Tough Choices: A Memoir.* New York: Portfolio.

Steinem, Gloria. (1993). *Revolution From Within.* Little, Brown and Company.

Williamson, Marianne. (1996). *A Return to Love: Reflections on the Principles of "A Course in Miracles." New York:* HarperCollins.

Yeung, Jessie. (2019, December 17). Global gender equality will take another 100 years to achieve, study finds. *CNN Business.* www.edition.cnn.com/2019/12/17/asia/gender-pay-gap-uk-wef-intl-hnk-scli/index.html.

Pew Research Center. (2020*). Worldwide Optimism About Future of Gender Equality, Even as Many See Advantages for Men.* www.pewresearch.org/global/2020/04/30/worldwide-optimism-about-future-of-gender-equality-even-as-many-see-advantages-for-men/.

About the Author

Brenda Landry is the President of Evoke Consulting Inc. She brings over 20 years of experience in consulting with a focus on leadership, communications, and executive advisory. She is a trusted authority to countless senior executives around the world.

Brenda was born in Halifax, N.S., and holds a Bachelor of Arts in psychology from Saint Mary's University and a Master of Business Administration in executive management consulting from Royal Roads University. A serendipitous fortune cookie her father handed her the night before he passed read, "If you've got it, flaunt it," which inspired the title of this book. Brenda lives in Toronto with her yellow lab Daisy.

www.ingramcontent.com/pod-product-compliance
Lightning Source LLC
Chambersburg PA
CBHW071449080526
44587CB00014B/2050